The Self Help Summary

A short guide to the key ideas and thinkers from the world of personal development

JOE REDSTON

Published by Ready Made Theatre Ltd
Copyright © Joe Redston 2018

The author asserts his moral right to be identified as the author of this book.

All rights reserved. No part of this publication may be reproduced, distributed, stored in or introduced into a retrieval system, or transmitted in any form or by any means, including photocopying, recording, or other electronic or mechanical methods, without the prior written permission of the publisher, except as permitted by the UK Copyright, Designs and Patents Act 1988.
For permission requests, contact:
readymadetheatre@gmail.com

Although every precaution has been taken to verify the accuracy of the information contained herein, the author and publisher assume no responsibility for errors or omissions. No liability is assumed for damages that may result from the use of information contained within.

CONTENTS

List of Resource Reviews	v
Author's Note	vii
CHAPTER 0 :: Introduction	1
CHAPTER 1 :: What Is Self-Help?	13
CHAPTER 2 :: Personal Responsibility	27
CHAPTER 3 :: Values	37
CHAPTER 4 :: Goal Setting	53
CHAPTER 5 :: Take Action	67
CHAPTER 6 :: Communication	95
CHAPTER 7 :: Leadership	107
CHAPTER 8 :: Tools & Tactics	123
CHAPTER 9 :: Next Steps	143
APPENDIX 1 :: 10-Point Action Plan	149
APPENDIX 2 :: 12 Books to Get You Started	151
About the Author	153
Acknowledgements	155

LIST OF RESOURCE REVIEWS

Alphabetically by title

'7 Habits of Highly Effective People, The' :: Stephen R. Covey :: P25
'Alchemist, The' :: Paulo Coelho :: P147
'Awaken the Giant Within' :: Anthony Robbins :: P24
'Commencement Speech' :: Admiral William H. McRaven :: P84
'Doing Good Better' :: William Macaskill :: P51
'Eat That Frog!' :: Brian Tracy :: P64
'Fear Setting' :: Tim Ferriss :: P60
'GaryVee Audio Experience, The' :: Gary Vaynerchuk :: P80
'Goals!' :: Brian Tracy :: P64
'Goal Setting V Processes' :: Scott Adams :: P62
'How to Win Friends and Influence People' :: Dale Carnegie :: P98
'Magic of Thinking Big, The' :: David Schwartz :: P55
'Man in the Arena, The' :: Theodore Roosevelt :: P116
'Man's Search for Meaning' :: Viktor Frankl :: P28
'Men Are from Mars, Women Are from Venus' :: John Gray :: P101
'Mindset' :: Dr Carol S. Dweck :: P11
'Nelson Mandela: Portrait of an Extraordinary Man' :: Richard Stengel :: P114
'Power of Now, The' :: Eckhart Tolle :: P79
'Richest Man in Babylon, The' :: George S. Clason :: P48
'Secret, The' :: Rhonda Byrne :: P139
'Seth's Blog' :: Seth Godin :: P45
'Seven Laws of Spiritual Success, The' :: Deepak Chopra :: P??34
'Start With Why' :: Simon Sinek :: P110
'Think and Grow Rich' :: Napoleon Hill :: P22
'Tools of Titans' :: Tim Ferris :: P141
'When to Quit' :: Chris Guillebeau :: P118
'Why Procrastinators Procrastinate' :: Tim Urban :: P74

Links to these, the other resources mentioned in the book, and lots of additional material can be found at:
   www.joeredston.com/shs/resources

AUTHOR'S NOTE

"Standing on the shoulders of giants" is a phrase that can be traced back at least as far as Bernard of Chartres, a 12th century French philosopher, which makes it relevant to this book in more ways than one. The thoughts it contains are the work of countless giants through the ages. I have simply gathered them in one place, in the hope that will be useful to people.

Where I have been able to find a clear origin for an idea, it is mentioned, but many of the concepts are referenced by so many different people that finding the original source can be tricky. I suspect that if we were able to look deeply enough, we could trace everything in this book way back into the mists of time …

To keep things simple, I have not used any footnotes or specific references in the text. If you are interested in the details, you can find them at my website:

www.joeredston.com/shs/references

CHAPTER 0 :: INTRODUCTION

I REMEMBER MY 40TH BIRTHDAY very clearly. I woke up in my parents' house, in the same room that I had as a teenager. I was living there at the time and basically broke, with few meaningful relationships, and very little going on that I was proud of. I looked in the mirror that morning and asked myself: "How have I ended up back here?"

I wasn't angry or bitter – a bit embarrassed, maybe, but life goes that way sometimes. Mainly, I was bewildered as to how I'd gone from seemingly having things pretty sorted – long-term relationship, nice house, work that I enjoyed – to essentially having to start my life over from the beginning.

I'd been studying self-help resources for a few years by that point, but that was the day I really engaged with the process. What followed was a journey of discovery. I read hundreds of books, took online courses, and watched or listened to thousands of hours of audio and video, absorbing some of the smartest and most practical thinking that human beings have ever done, from Confucius to Stephen R. Covey. But this book isn't about my story – it's about the things I've learned from these great thinkers.

Before we start, I need to make sure you don't get the wrong idea – this stuff is a lot easier to learn and write about than it is to actually do. I've made some real progress in the last few years, but don't think for one second that I am some perfectly oiled machine that gets through every single day with maximum efficiency, achieving all my goals exactly on schedule, with a life full of idyllic relationships. That is absolutely not where I'm at. I've still got plenty of things to work on – I have days (occasionally even weeks…) that disappear in a haze of procrastination, there are relationships that I know I need to work harder on, and I definitely still look at myself in the mirror sometimes and ask "Why did I do that?!"

But I am making progress, and it's down to the concepts and thinkers in this book.

My hope is that if you ever have one of those days where you look in the mirror and find yourself asking "Why?", the information and ideas in these pages might help you to find *your* answer.

ABOUT THIS BOOK

It goes by lots of names – self–help, personal development, self–development, self–education … you may have heard other expressions, depending on your age and where in the world you are. Whichever term you use, my intention is to give you an overview of the principles involved, and an introduction to some of the key thinkers and their work. I hope this will inspire you to begin your own self–development journey, and give you some ideas on where to go next.

Before we get in to that, there are a few things I'd like you to bear in mind.

TIMING

"When the student is ready, the teacher will appear." Chinese proverb

In the end, your personal development comes down to, well, you. No-one else can do it for you. And in the end, you will do it when the time is right for you. There's a famous commencement speech JK Rowling gave at Harvard in 2008 where she talks about the process involved in becoming one of the most successful authors of all time. In it, she talks about some of her early struggles, and says that "rock bottom became the solid foundation upon which I rebuilt my life." You may not be at rock bottom (I sincerely hope you aren't), but for you to make any significant changes, the chances are you probably need to be at least a little bit uncomfortable in at least a couple of areas of your life. If that isn't you right now, then that's brilliant. Hopefully you will still find this book interesting and informative – but it may not be for you right now. However, if you are feeling a bit dissatisfied in one or more areas of your life, then this could be the time to start making some changes. Know that the answers are out there, you just need to go and find them.

LEARNING

"The only learning that's mattered is what I got on my own, doing what I want to do." Richard Bach, 20th century American author

Getting the most from this book will involve learning some new ideas, and doing some work. Let me firstly reassure you that we aren't talking about going back to school here!

If your memories of school are not particularly happy, can I ask you to please put that to one side. Although you need to be open to the idea of learning new skills, the areas we'll be looking at aren't the ones that school tested so you might surprise yourself. On the other hand, if you found the academic side of things easy at school, you may find that the ideas in this book challenge you in different ways.

Either way, please be patient – with the book, with the concepts it contains, and with yourself. Please approach your self-education journey with a growth mindset, rather than a fixed mindset. (See P11).

LANGUAGE

There's a possibility that phrases like 'growth mindset' or 'self-education journey' make you roll your eyes or grimace in disgust. Throughout this book, you will read words like journey, inspire, and spiritual, but please don't let the language put you off. If that sort of language makes you feel uncomfortable, I know why – I used to feel exactly the same way.

When any of us enter a new world, there is a language barrier of some sort to overcome. If you take up a new sport, you need to learn the jargon – you need someone to explain the offside rule, or the difference between the baseline and service line. The same is true in business – at first, talk of CEOs and USPs and KPIs can be bewildering, but once you're familiar with the terms, it all makes sense. What can make it worse is when people use jargon to try and emphasise their superiority, or to make someone else feel small or stupid. Most of us have been on the receiving end of that at some point in our lives, and it's not a pleasant experience.

There's not too much in the way of jargon in this book, but there are words and phrases that come pre-loaded with meaning. If an idea like 'goal setting' makes you want to immediately throw this book away because you associate it with wishy-washy inspirational quotes on Facebook, then – I hear you.

In addition to the mentors (there's another potentially troublesome word!) that I will write about, there are other people out there jumping on the personal development bandwagon who don't have much integrity. In certain areas, this has given personal development rather a bad name – many people associate it with spaced-out 'gurus' who charge a lot of money but don't actually know what they are talking about. They write books and blog posts that are meaningless waffle. We won't be going there.

The principles and people we'll be talking about are the ones that have proved their worth, and stood the test of time – many of them over thousands of years. But they do use words like journey, inspire and spiritual. Please keep your mind open to the ideas, and don't let uncomfortable words put you off.

"The menu is not the meal." Alan Watts, 20th century British philosopher

CLICHES

Many of the ideas in this book are thousands of years old, and some of them have become cliches. This can make it easy to dismiss them as irrelevant, but again, I would ask you to keep an open mind. A cliche is defined in the Collins dictionary as "a word or expression that has lost much of its force through overexposure." Note that it doesn't say that the word or expression isn't true or meaningful, only that its impact has been diluted through overuse. When you encounter a concept in this book that seems like a bit of a cliche, look closely at it, for this is often where we can learn the most. Cliches become cliches because they are true.

COMFORT ZONE

"The shell must break before the bird can fly." Lord Alfred Tennyson, 19th century British poet

"He who is not courageous enough to take risks will accomplish nothing in life." Muhammed Ali, 20th century American boxer

See what I mean about language and cliches? 'Comfort Zone'. Language doesn't get more cliched than that!

Simply put, your comfort zone is the things you do all the time. It's always going to the same supermarket for the weekly shop, ordering the same coffee at lunch, buying the famous brand of trainers, or watching the same TV show as everyone else so you can join in the conversation at work – all those little habits and actions that make us feel part of a tribe. Sometimes this can be a good thing – maybe you've made some great friends at your gym, or enjoy guessing the next plot twist on the latest hit TV show.

However, in order to get better at anything – to learn, to grow – we need to step outside of our comfort zones – to make changes, to do things differently ... but that's a really hard thing to do. When we are inside our comfort zone, we feel safe. Stepping out of our comfort zone is intimidating. It means taking a risk. But it also means we have a chance to improve our lives – to make things better. There will probably be bits of this book that make you feel uncomfortable as you read them. That's a *good* thing – it means you're outside of your comfort zone, and that means you're learning. You absolutely do not have to agree with every idea that is covered ... but if you're feeling challenged by something, don't immediately dismiss it – and be sure to ask yourself why you feel that way.

Let's use Alex as an example. She has a job that she's

been doing long enough to cope with any of the problems that might arise. Rarely does Alex find herself in a position where she doesn't have the answer. She is firmly inside her comfort zone. But that is where her problem lies. Although Alex quite likes her job at the moment, because she's not pushing herself eventually she'll get bored, or someone else will overtake her. She stagnates, and the job she used to love becomes a tedious chore.

Maybe this sounds familiar to you. Or – even worse – maybe you never really liked your job in the first place. If that's the case then boredom can turn into outright loathing. You resent doing the work, you bicker with your colleagues, you hate your boss – everything about your job sucks (hopefully this isn't you, by the way). In this situation, it might be time to leave your comfort zone.

This idea of stepping out of your comfort zone is one of the most important concepts to grasp – one that has the potential to have a massive impact on your life. Start small – order a different coffee tomorrow, or walk the kids home from school by a different route. It might end up being a bad choice, but you need to test the boundaries. Make sure that your decisions are the best ones, not just the easy ones.

There's a good chance that as you're reading, the ideas that make you feel the most uncomfortable are the ones that will ultimately benefit you the most.

RESOURCES

Throughout the book, I have included reviews of books, videos, podcasts, blogs, and other resources that you might find useful. These range from personal development classics, like 'Think and Grow Rich', to more contemporary thinkers. It's not possible to cover everything, and everyone has a different opinion on what the most important resources are, but the ones I've included have either stood the test of time, or currently have an enormous following.

What I've tried to do is give you an introduction to all the different 'flavours' of personal development. This ranges

CHAPTER 0 :: Introduction

from the more spiritual work of Eckhart Tolle, to straight talkers like Gary Vaynerchuk. There's the philosophy of Lao Tzu, and the more practical approach of someone like Tim Ferriss. Chances are, you won't like all of them – some will resonate with you more than others.

We've already talked about how important timing can be. There have been books that made a huge impression on me that I enthusiastically recommend to a friend ... who hates it! Similarly, I've been bored to tears by a book that everyone else considers amazing. This brings us to a crucial point: If something you are reading/watching/listening to isn't connecting with you for some reason – put it to one side. Look for something else that you *do* engage with. Life is too short to labour through a 300–page 'classic' that you aren't enjoying. Don't throw it away though! There have been a few times I've returned to a book that didn't originally grab me ... and because I've changed in the intervening months and years, my response to the book changes too. After originally dismissing something, I now find it deeply connects with me.

You need to invest in your self–education. This primarily means time, but probably involves a bit of money, too. There's a huge amount of free resources around these days – particularly some of the incredible podcasts out there – and if you're looking for books, they can often be picked up second–hand on Amazon for a couple of pounds. Skip one latte a week, and invest that money in yourself.

Your time investment doesn't need to be huge, either. If you can read ten pages of a good book every day, you'll get through the list of 12 books on P151 in about a year. If you do nothing else, using your ten pages a day to read those 12 books will put you in a radically different place in a year's time.

GET A JOURNAL

Tools and Tactics are covered in Chapter 8, but I want to mention your journal here as it is the most important tool you'll have. Your journal isn't a diary. While you might use it to record private thoughts, it is primarily a place to jot down quotes that you like (maybe at the back for easy reference?), to summarise a great TED talk, or to take notes from an inspiring podcast interview. Our memories are rarely as reliable as we think, so take good notes. There's an old cliche that says it's better to have a short pencil than a long memory.

If you don't already have a journal, get yourself an empty notebook and a pen, and have it handy as you're reading this book. It doesn't need to be anything fancy at this point.

Let's christen it. On the first page, write out this question: Why did I start reading 'The Self-Help Summary'?

And underneath, take a few minutes to write your answer – as honestly as you can.

ABOUT ME

None of the ideas in this book are mine. What I've tried to do is distil the concepts that I've seen repeated again and again, and gather them all in one place in the hope that it provides you with a useful summary. It's important for you to know that my personal development journey only started in earnest a few years before I wrote this book. In some ways, I'm not really qualified for the job. I haven't spent decades guiding and coaching thousands of people, and I've definitely still got a long way to go on my own journey. Some of the things I write about I've been able to implement pretty effectively ... but others ... well, let's just say I understand the principle, but applying it in practice is proving to be a bit trickier!

With that confession out of the way, I also think that my being relatively new to the self-development adventure and not having mastered all the concepts, puts me in a really good position to write this book. I can clearly remember what it feels like to come across an idea that makes sense, to then try and do it ... and fall flat on my face. I remember what it felt like the first time I picked up a personal development book (it was 'The Richest Man in Babylon', by the way. See P48 for details), or the first time I put an educational CD in the car rather than listen to sports radio (Jim Rohn's 'How to Live an Exceptional Life'). I recall the trepidation I felt, the sense of nervousness – bordering on embarrassment – at what other people might think if they found out I was reading and listening to this stuff. Maybe some of the experts have forgotten what that feels like. Let me assure you that I haven't. I know just how close you are to putting this book of touchy–feely mumbo–jumbo down, and never picking it up again.

Having said all of that, I have read hundreds of books and absorbed thousands of hours of audio and video content. I'm far enough into my journey to be seeing some real, tangible benefits from the ideas I've learned – I know they work. Like I said, I don't pretend to be implementing all the ideas in this book and sailing through life achieving all my wildest dreams ... but I am working on it. And I can truly say that the ideas in this book have changed my life for the better. I hope they help you in the same way.

DEALING WITH CHANGE

"If you keep doing what you've always done, you'll keep getting what you've always got." Zig Ziglar, 20th century American author

"For things to change for you, you have to change." Jim Rohn, 20th century American author

The first time I came across the Zig Ziglar quote above, it hit me like a ton of bricks. While there was nothing particularly wrong in my life, I'd been doing the same things for a decade or more but was expecting things to somehow magically change for me. Shortly after reading the Ziglar quote, I came across the one from Jim Rohn.

And with that, the fog finally lifted. It was understanding the connection between these two quotes that finally made me realise I had work to do. If I wanted to alter the course of my life, I needed to start doing things differently – I needed to change. As human beings though, we are all hardwired to be resistant to change. It comes back to our comfort zones – we want things to be the same, to be safe and predictable ... but ... if – like I had – you've got a little voice somewhere inside wondering "Is this it?", then you need to get comfortable with being uncomfortable. Understand that you're going to need to make changes, that there are going to be challenges along the way, and that the path won't always be smooth.

To get through this, we need to adopt a growth mindset towards change.

HOW TO READ THIS BOOK

Reading it from start to finish will undoubtedly pay dividends, and I hope that eventually you do read all of it. But at the beginning, there might be certain ideas and concepts that stretch you more than you expect – they take you too far out of your comfort zone. That's OK. Skip that bit, and come back to it another day. Feel free to dip in and out, and to begin with only read the bits that grab your attention.

There is an important caveat to this though. If a certain idea is making you particularly uncomfortable, there's a good chance that concept is the one which will have the most profound impact on your life. Ask yourself why it made you uncomfortable. What is it about that particular person or idea that you find challenging? Mark the page and leave it for another day, but make sure you come back to it at some point.

Speaking of marking the page, I urge you to read this book with a pencil or highlighter close by. Underline bits you like, cross out bits you don't, make notes in the margins, list your favourite pages inside the front cover so you can easily find them again, start a list of the resources that interest you inside the back cover – make the book yours. Your personal development adventure is uniquely yours, and it starts here.

"The journey of a thousand miles begins with a single step." Lao Tzu, Chinese philosopher, 5th century BCE

'Mindset' [2006]
Dr Carol S. Dweck
SUMMARY: Fairly easy to read, research–based approach with lots of examples.
KEY QUOTE: "Everyone can change and grow through application and experience."

Taking the first steps towards self–education can be incredibly challenging. The main reason for this is usually rooted in fear that we won't succeed, that we won't be good enough, that we will expose our inadequacy to the world. But what if we could change our thinking? What if we could put ourselves in a position where we look at all aspects of our lives as an opportunity for growth?

Dr Carol Dweck wrote a fantastic book called, simply, 'Mindset'. She is a psychologist who has spent decades studying the power of people's beliefs. Her research has demonstrated "how a simple belief about yourself…guides a large part of your life".

In the book, Dweck explains how there are two basic mindsets – fixed, and growth. When we have a fixed mindset about something, we believe that our ability in a particular area reaches a limit at a certain point. For many years I had a fixed mindset regarding maths. At school, I was fortunate to find GCSE maths fairly easy to understand. But when I moved to A–Level, it was a completely different story. I found it way more challenging, and gave up within a matter of weeks. Until I read 'Mindset', I believed that I had reached my 'ceiling' with maths at GCSE standard. I thought I had a certain ability for maths that just ran out at A–Level. I had a fixed mindset towards Maths.

The other mindset we can have is one of growth. I play the drums, and have always had a growth mindset towards them. At the age of 38, I found a teacher who showed me a whole new way to play.

He pushed me hard, challenging my thinking about every aspect of playing the drums. I loved every minute of it, and made significant improvements. I had a growth mindset towards learning drums.

Dweck tells us that while we might start with certain natural abilities in certain areas, there is nothing that we can't improve upon. Admittedly, some areas require more application than others – I have more natural talent for drumming than for maths, for example – but there is no area in which we can't improve if we so choose. This applies to all areas of life – from reading to playing football, from driving to DIY, from parenting to listening – these are all skills that every single one of us can improve ... *if* we approach them with a growth mindset.

In what areas of life do you have a growth mindset? Where are you continually improving?

Perhaps more importantly ... in what areas do you have a fixed mindset? Is this holding you back at all?

(This would be a really good time to make two lists in your journal ...)

If some of the ideas in this book seem difficult or alien, I urge you to adopt a growth mindset and not to give up at the first hurdle.

Begin with asking yourself a simple question:

Where are the opportunities for me to grow today?

"One can choose to go back toward safety or forward toward growth. Growth must be chosen again and again; fear must be overcome again and again." Abraham Maslow, 20th century American psychologist

MORE LIKE THIS: 'Self Renewal' by John W. Gardner, 'Daring Greatly' by Brené Brown

CHAPTER 1 :: WHAT IS SELF-HELP?

DEFINING SELF-HELP

"Self–help is a load of drippy–hippy mumbo–jumbo invented by dishonest, money-grabbing scumbags to scam gullible idiots".

At least, that's what I used to think.

But when I opened my mind – and it was just the tiniest amount to begin with – I learned that self–improvement is something human beings have worked at since the beginning of time.

There's a very clear line in personal development that runs from current writers like Seth Godin and Tim Urban, back to Jim Rohn and Stephen R. Covey. Before them were Napoleon Hill and Dale Carnegie, and we can then trace self–development all the way back to Seneca, Confucius and beyond.

As I studied the work of these great writers and thinkers, I realised that certain themes and ideas have been repeated across the ages. The words are slightly different, but the ideas are the same. Concepts like taking responsibility for your decisions and actions, the importance of knowing what you stand for, having a clear idea of where you want to get to, and connecting with people around you. The greatest minds in history have all arrived at the same conclusions – that there is a set of fundamental principles that guide human behaviour and achievement. The wisest human beings that have ever lived talk about the same foundational ideas, and that suggests to me that it's probably a good idea to try and live according to these concepts. We are talking about principles like honesty, kindness, courage, patience and integrity, which can be summarised by the Golden Rule:

"What you do not want done to yourself, do not do to others."

Those words were written by Confucius in the 6th century BCE, and a variation of this appears in all the major philosophical schools that we know of, so it seems wise to pay attention to it (see P39 for more on the Golden Rule). A good way to think about it is to imagine the opposite. Imagine someone who lives their life dishonestly, acting with cruelty and selfishness at all times. It is obvious that this is not a person we would want to spend much time with! The message repeated time and again throughout human history is that we should not fight these principles – to do so is ultimately futile. Personal development is essentially the process of understanding these ideas more fully, and deciding how to use them on a day to day basis in order to lead a richer, more fulfilled life.

Personal development is a journey – it is our attempt to live by these fundamental principles. It is a fascinating and exciting journey, but one which can be really hard to start. There's a bit more bad news, too – you never reach your destination! Every time you think you might be getting close, you uncover another layer. The good news is that each layer brings more understanding and is more fulfilling than the last. Self–development is a commitment to a process of continual improvement, in all areas of your life, for the rest of your life. There are no quick fixes, and please don't believe anyone who tells you otherwise.

As you begin this book, you might be a bit cynical about self–development (like I was), or perhaps just a bit overwhelmed and unsure where to start. To try and help with that, this book has three main objectives:

1. Summarise the most important concepts and thinkers.

2. Provide you with some basic knowledge and understanding.

3. Inspire you to dig a little deeper.

The road to the life you really want to lead involves some

learning. Please don't let that put you off! It's not like being at school, primarily because you get to choose the things you want to work on. If you are honest with yourself, you probably already know the areas where you feel you could make some improvements. You can choose to focus on the stuff that really helps *you*. That doesn't mean to say it will always be easy – sometimes you will have to dig really deep – but if you keep taking those small steps every single day, then you will see progress.

"If you can't fly, then run. If you can't run, then walk. If you can't walk, then crawl. But whatever you do, you have to keep moving forward." Martin Luther King Jr, 20th century American activist

THERE'S NOTHING NEW

"Each truth you learn will be, for you, as new as if it had never been written." Inscribed on the Temple of Luxor, Ancient Egyptian, around 14th century BCE

As I started to immerse myself in the huge variety of resources that are available, one thing kept jumping out at me – the fact that I kept coming across the same fundamental ideas, repeated time and again, all throughout history. The language and delivery changes, but some of the smartest human beings that have ever walked this Earth have all arrived at the same basic conclusions: that our role here is to live the best life we can, and the way to do that is actually pretty simple. Almost 2500 years ago, Plato said:

> *"Good people do not need laws to tell them to act responsibly, while bad people will find a way around the laws."*

Around 500 years after Plato, Marcus Aurelius wrote:

> *"Waste no more time arguing about what a good man should be. Be one."*

I almost feel like I can tell you to stop reading right here. The truth is that deep down, we already know what we should be doing ... however, we also know that living the best life we can is much easier said than done, so if you'd like some tools and tactics to help you be the person you want to be, then keep reading …

As you do, you will notice how a tool like goal setting (for example) has been talked about for thousands of years. It seems to me that if everyone from Aristotle ("Man is a goal setting machine") to Longfellow ("If you would hit the mark, you must aim a little above it") to Einstein ("If you want to live a happy life, tie it to a goal") thinks that having clearly defined goals is a good idea … well, then it probably is. I for one am certainly not going to argue with them!

All the concepts in this book are like that. They have been discussed and written about for centuries, so perhaps they are more than just good ideas? Perhaps they are fundamental principles that we can all use to navigate our way more effectively through the glorious chaos that is life on Earth?

Remember also that no single source can provide you with everything you personally need … this book is just the beginning.

"The secret of change is to focus all of your energy, not on fighting the old, but on building the new." Socrates, Ancient Greek philosopher, 5th century BCE

THE ORIGINS OF SELF-HELP

"Know thyself." Inscribed on the Temple of Apollo in Ancient Greece, around 4th century BCE

For almost as long as people have been able to write things down, we have been writing about what it means to be human, and how we might get better at it.

One of the earliest known manuscripts, the Huangdi Sijing (or 'Yellow Emperor's Four Classics'), opens with this passage:

> *"The Way generates standards. Standards serve as marking cords to demarcate success and failure and are what clarify*

CHAPTER 1 :: What Is Self-Help?

the crooked and the straight. Therefore, those who hold fast to the Way generate standards and do not to dare to violate them; having established standards, they do not dare to discard them."

Huangdi is telling us that 'standards' – or 'principles' – are what keep us on the straight and narrow, and that we can't ignore them. Your Gran was probably the same – it's likely you can remember her saying something along the lines of:

"If you can't say anything nice, don't say anything at all."

Turns out, your Gran knew what she was talking about! One of the earliest known Sumerian texts, 'The Instructions of Shuruppak', contains this line:

"Insults and stupid speaking receive the attention of the land."

Your Gran got her wisdom from King Suruppak. Both he and Huangdi lived at roughly the same time – around 2600 BCE. That's over 4500 years ago. So why are so many of us still not heeding this timeless advice? These ideas – and others like them – have endured for millennia. Instead of fighting them or denying them, let's instead understand the incredible impact these ideas can have on the world.

Personal development can help us with this. It can restore our confidence, get us up off our backsides, show us how to communicate better with the people around us, and ultimately enable us to live happier and more fulfilling lives.

The information is already out there, waiting for us. All we have to do is go find it.

Are you ready to start looking?

"The most important knowledge is that which guides the way you lead your life." Seneca, Roman philosopher, 1st century

THE PROBLEMS WITH SELF-HELP

There's no doubt that at certain times, in certain areas, with certain people, the idea of self improvement has not been considered a worthwhile investment of time.

It's likely that part of your brain is thinking that right now. And that is a good thing. You absolutely should maintain a healthy scepticism about everything you see, hear and read. Not just in the pages of this book, but in your life generally. Technically, facts should be indisputable, but it rarely turns out that way because there can be huge variation in the way that people interpret those facts. This applies to everything from election results, to arguments between people over whose turn it is to take the rubbish out. There are always at least two sides to every story – whether you like it or not.

Broadly speaking, the central ideas in personal development have stayed constant for thousands of years. (If you want to skip the rest of the book – here's a clue: it boils down to one central maxim ... be nice). But those ideas have been interpreted in a myriad of different ways. You have the research–based approach of people like Carol Dweck or Napoleon Hill, who interviewed hundreds of people over the course of 20 years before writing 'Think and Grow Rich'. You have the practical, hands–on methodology of people who have been there and done that, like Tim Ferris or Viktor

CHAPTER 1 :: What Is Self-Help?

Frankl, whose seminal 'Man's Search For Meaning' is based on his personal experiences in Nazi death camps. Then as a contrast to that, you have the spiritual, inspirational approach of Eckart Tolle or Paulo Coelho.

The problems tend to arise when people are introduced to personal development, and someone recommends the wrong sort of material to them. Ultimately, it's a good thing to be be familiar with a wide range of thinkers, ideas and styles, but it's best to start with something that feels right to you. A book like 'The Secret' can sell millions of copies in a very short space of time – but it absolutely won't be for everyone. If 'The Secret' is not for you then that's fine – but that doesn't mean you should dismiss all the other resources on the assumption they will be the same. They most certainly are not. So please be patient, and don't attach too much importance to someone else's opinion.

The other big problem that personal development has is that too many people think there is some sort of miracle cure or quick fix out there. This is absolutely a mistake I made. I went through a stage of devouring as much information as I possibly could, thinking that it was only a matter of time before I found the one book or video that was going to solve all my problems and change my life in one afternoon. Unfortunately, it doesn't work like that. What I eventually realised was that I was using the constant search for new information as an excuse for not actually doing any of the work. I was looking for a shortcut. There isn't one.

If you want things to change, you're going to have to put the work in.

(I'm going to say that a lot – and I'm not going to apologise for it).

When you get down to it, none of the people I've met who claim that personal development is a load of rubbish have actually done any of the work involved. So when you hear people claiming that self-education is a mug's game, take a close look at them, and see how much *work* they have done.

The problems aren't with the thinkers or their ideas.

SOME NOTES ON ANCIENT THINKERS

From the east ...

There are two main writers here – Confucius and Lao Tzu. Living so long ago, they both have slightly hazy backgrounds and it's hard to be certain on the details of their lives. No one is really sure how much of what has been handed down was actually written by them, and how much was written by their followers in later years.

There is also the problem of translation. The Chinese languages contain words that simply don't have Western equivalents, so you will frequently come across variations in the wording of their quotes.

Neither of these two things really matter, however. Instead, focus on how people from so long ago had the same basic needs, wants and desires as we do today, and how they looked to fulfil those needs.

If you're interested in digging a bit deeper into Eastern philosophy, I recommend starting with Ursula Le Guin's translation of the 'Tao Te Ching'.

From the west ...

For any academics out there, please forgive me – I'm going to lump all the Greek and Roman writers and thinkers into one big group! This covers everyone from Heraclitus to Marcus Aurelius and beyond – which covers a huge array of philosophical ideas and concepts.

There is a lot more known about the Greeks and Romans than the Chinese, so we can be more confident about who said what, and exactly what they meant. However, this book is an introduction, so we do not need to worry ourselves with the details.

If you're interested in this area and want to read an original text, I suggest starting with Seneca's 'Letters from a Stoic'. In the meantime, simply notice how relevant their words still are, thousands of years after they were written.

From religion ...

Many years ago, I took part in a cycling trip across Cuba. Over 50 people from all walks of life met for the first time at Heathrow airport. On our first night together in Havana, I looked around at the group and was astonished to see everyone talking and laughing together. I mentioned to the lady next to me how amazing I thought this was, and being older and wiser than me, she gave a little laugh. "You wait," she said. "In a few days, someone will bring up either politics or religion. We'll see how friendly it stays after that!"

Sure enough, a couple of days later a recent election result came up in conversation. Within minutes the dynamic of the group had irrevocably changed.

I've managed to avoid politics in this book (I hope) ... and I thought long and hard about whether to mention religion in any context.

Whatever your personal views towards Buddha, Jesus, Mohammed or any of the other historical figures associated with the religions of the world, there is no doubt that they have had a profound influence on our culture.

What is also clear – and important, from the perspective of this book – is that the idea of the Golden Rule (to treat others as you wish to be treated) appears in nearly every religious and ethical tradition that we know of. The earliest record of it dates back around 4000 years to the Ancient Egyptian story of 'The Eloquent Peasant'.

I have occasionally quoted from religious texts and figures, mainly to demonstrate how the same ideas appear all through history, and all around the world.

IN CONCLUSION

For our purposes, the details of exactly when Lao Tzu was born, or whether Plato was really quoting Socrates directly or not aren't too important – we'll let the academics figure that out! What we do know is that the writings and concepts associated with these thinkers have been handed down over the course of thousands of years. When something hangs around for so long, the chances are it contains valuable information that is probably worth paying attention to. These ancient ideas formed the foundation of modern thinking, and thus form the basis of our continued self-education.

These people – and many others like them in the intervening years – gave their entire lives over to figuring out the best way to live. They have done the work for us. Let's be grateful for that – and let's not let their work be wasted.

> **'Think and Grow Rich' [1937]**
> *Napoleon Hill*
> SUMMARY: Old fashioned language; a long, challenging read, but worth the effort.
> KEY QUOTE: "Both poverty and riches are the offspring of thought".
>
> This is the grandaddy of 20th century personal development books. It took Hill over 20 years to interview more than 500 of the most successful people of the time including Andrew Carnegie, Henry Ford and Thomas Edison. The book has now sold over 70 million copies, demonstrating that the lessons and advice it contains are as valid now as they ever were. It's pretty long, and was published in 1937 so the style is very different to more modern books. This can make the ideas hard to follow at times. It is ultimately worth the effort, but it's a long, challenging read compared to someone like Brian Tracy, so bear that in mind if you decide to give this one a go. It's probably best not to make this one the first personal development book you read!
>
> In terms of the book's message, the most important thing to understand is that Hill says being 'rich' is about a lot more than just money. In order of importance, to be truly rich in life the first thing he says we need is a positive mental attitude (see P136). His list also includes 'sound physical health', 'the hope of future achievement', and 'an open mind

towards all subjects for all people'. Last on his list is 'financial security', and as Hill himself said, "note with great benefit that money comes at the end of the list". The book then explains the 13 steps that will lead a person to be rich in all areas of life. Read it for the details, but Hill essentially says that you need to state clearly what is it you want, go after it in a consistent, persistent manner, and banish negative thoughts from your mind.

There are two other important concepts he covers that don't get mentioned very often in self-improvement books. The first of these is his concept of the 'mastermind'. Hill states that when we surround ourselves with smart people, the combined brain power of the group enables everyone to achieve more than they would on their own. Basically – get yourself a good team! Learning which people to surround yourself with is a crucial skill. (See 'People' on P129).

Hill also writes more extensively than most about what he calls 'the Sixth Sense'. For many years this was seen as a very 'unscientific' view, but there has been some recent research that suggests trusting your gut instinct might not be such a bad thing. It definitely shouldn't be the only thing you listen to, but next time you get that uncomfortable feeling in the pit of your stomach, Napoleon Hill (and a fair few 21st century scientists) would say that it might be worth asking yourself why it's there.

This is one of the classics of the personal development world, and you'll get out of it what you put in.

"The only thing we have power over in the universe is our thoughts." René Descartes, 17th century French philosopher

MORE LIKE THIS: 'As a Man Thinketh' by James Allen, 'Pushing to the Front' by Orison Swett Marden

'Awaken the Giant Within' [1991]
Anthony (Tony) Robbins

SUMMARY: Direct, motivational style; long, with masses of practical advice.

KEY QUOTE: "It is in your moments of decision that your destiny is shaped."

Robbins is perhaps the largest character in the contemporary self-help world. He runs massive seminars around the world attended by tens of thousands of people each year, and has a huge celebrity following. His style is very distinctive; direct – almost evangelical – and perhaps not to everyone's taste. A quick YouTube search will give you a feel for his delivery.

Whatever you might think about his methods, underneath it all is some incredibly good content. He has so much material available – books, audio, video, live events – that he could easily be the only resource you ever turn to!

'Awaken the Giant Within' is detailed, motivational, and covers a huge range of subjects. Robbins' main message is that your mental state drives everything else, and when you get that sorted your life can really start to open up. It's not just about motivation – each chapter ends with some practical, actionable steps that you can take. The third section of the book is called 'Seven Days to Shape Your Life', and outlines a week long program you can follow to start the process of 'awakening the giant within'. Of course, it takes a lot longer than seven days to see any lasting change, but Robbins is rooted in solid ideas – and he's been producing top quality content for decades. He coaches and advises some of the most successful people on the planet – and we can all get access to that same information for the price of a second-hand book!

"The only person you are destined to become is the person you decide to be." Ralph Waldo Emerson, 19th century American philosopher

MORE LIKE THIS: 'Laws of Success' by Les Brown, 'Flow' by Mihaly Csikszentmihalyi

'The 7 Habits of Highly Effective People' [1989]
Stephen R. Covey
SUMMARY: Gentle style; systematic, practical, principle-based approach.
KEY QUOTE: "Principled solutions stand in stark contrast to the common practices and thinking of our popular culture."

'7 Habits' wasn't the first personal development book I read, but it was the one that made me realise that self-improvement was a lifelong challenge, and that it was down to me how my life turns out. It's the book that turned my life around.

It was written in the 1980s, and some of the language and terms Covey uses have now become cliches, and are regularly parodied. When he talks about the Circle of Concern or your Circle of Influence, it's hard not to think of Robert De Niro in the film 'Meet the Fockers'! If you can put that image to one side, the concept of Concern vs Influence is one of the most important in the book. Briefly, your Circle of Concern is everything that you know about, including all the really big stuff like war, politics, climate change, and so on – the things we usually feel powerless to affect. Your Circle of Influence is smaller, and is the stuff you can directly affect with your actions. Covey tells us to focus on where we can influence things, and not to get bogged down worrying about all the big stuff. Excellent advice.

There are numerous concepts covered in this

amazing book, but the actual '7 Habits' are:
1. BE PROACTIVE. Accept personal responsibility, and take action.
2. BEGIN WITH THE END IN MIND. Understand your core values.
3. PUT FIRST THINGS FIRST. Set goals in alignment with your values.
4. THINK WIN/WIN. Work towards a mutually beneficial common goal.
5. SEEK FIRST TO UNDERSTAND, THEN TO BE UNDERSTOOD. Listen first, before giving your opinion.
6. SYNERGISE. Work with people, and allow them to use their skills and strengths.
7. SHARPEN THE SAW. Be constantly working to improve your body, mind and spirit.

Covey goes into great depth on each of the Habits, and woven into them are lots of other hugely important ideas. It's a detailed book, that really needs to be read a few times to get the most from it. You might find it heavy going at first, but persevere, and you will reap the benefits in all areas of your life.

There is also an audio available with Covey himself reading an abridged version of the book. It's excellent, and is an easier place to start getting familiar with the ideas that underly 'The 7 Habits of Highly Effective People'.

"In matters of style, swim with the current; in matters of principle, stand like a rock." Thomas Jefferson, one of the Founding Fathers of America, 18th century

MORE LIKE THIS: 'The Score Takes Care of Itself' by Bill Walsh, 'The Slight Edge' by Jeff Olson

CHAPTER 2 :: PERSONAL RESPONSIBILITY

"Work on yourself first. Take responsibility for your own progress."
The I Ching ['Book of Changes'], China, 4th–10th century BCE

"Man is affected not by events but by the view he takes of them."
Seneca, Roman philosopher, 1st century AD

"Whatever happens, take responsibility." Tony Robbins, 21st century American author

THE MORNING OF MY 40TH birthday in that bedroom at my parents' house was when it finally dawned on me – it was all my responsibility. The answer to the question "How have I ended up here?" was (and still is) "Because of the decisions I have made." I'd been reading self-development books intently for a few years at that point, and was familiar with the idea of accepting personal responsibility for my decisions. But that was the day I finally realised that the way my life had turned out was a consequence of the decisions I'd made in the past. The responsibility for my life is mine.

In retrospect, I feel a bit stupid for not making that connection earlier. I had engaged intellectually with the concept outlined in Viktor Frankl's brilliant book, 'Man's Search For Meaning' – I was even enjoying the power that I felt it gave me over my choices – but I hadn't engaged with it emotionally. When confronted with an awkward situation, I was getting better at thinking "OK, this could go a couple of ways here. It might be best if I handle it calmly, rather than rising to the bait", but it wasn't until that morning that I started really assessing where I was in life and understanding that it was all my responsibility.

The same is true for you. We're talking about taking absolute responsibility for the things you can control. Your choices. Your actions. Your decisions. Those are the things that determine YOUR life.

'Man's Search for Meaning' [1946]
Viktor E. Frankl
SUMMARY: A short guide to maintaining hope, no matter what.

KEY QUOTE: "Everything can be taken from a man but one thing: the last of the human freedoms – to choose one's attitude in any given set of circumstances, to choose one's own way."

When we talk about personal responsibility, there is a fine line between understanding that you have control over your decisions, but not blaming yourself for the challenges that might come your way. This is brilliantly expressed by Viktor Frankl in his classic 'Man's Search for Meaning.'

Frankl was an Austrian psychologist who was imprisoned in Auschwitz during World War II. While he was there, suffering some of the worst deprivations imaginable, he tried to work out why some people survived and others didn't. Eventually, he realised that it was down to their mindset. The ones who survived had something to live for – they didn't lose hope, they didn't give up. The survivors understood that even though their liberty and dignity were utterly destroyed, they were still able to choose their response, no matter how terrible the situation became. They understood that their ability to choose – what Frankl calls "the last of the human freedoms" – was what made them able to survive.

This short book isn't the most comfortable read, as it does contain a first-hand account of life in a Nazi death camp. While Frankl doesn't go into graphic detail on how they were treated – the book won't give you nightmares or anything – he does write about those experiences in a very matter-of-fact manner. Even more importantly, the book contains perhaps the most vital lesson any of us need to learn – one that can be incredibly empowering.

> We don't always have control over what happens to us, but we always have the freedom to choose how we respond. Admittedly, sometimes the amount of time we have to choose is incredibly small ... but there is always a choice to be made. And that decision is ours, and ours alone.
>
> *"It's not what happens to you, but how you react to it that matters." Epictetus, Roman philosopher, 1st century*
>
> MORE LIKE THIS: 'Jonathan Livingstone Seagull' by Richard Bach, 'Long Walk to Freedom' by Nelson Mandela

MAINTAINING BALANCE

There is a balance to be kept here. If you choose (and it is – of course – your choice) to agree with Frankl's ideas, it's really important that as well as taking responsibility for the decisions you've made that didn't work out quite as you hoped, you also understand that all the good things that have happened in your life are also a result of your choices. Taking responsibility doesn't just mean we beat ourselves up when things don't quite go to plan. We are also allowed to be proud of our successes.

Another important aspect of this is to understand that sometimes things happen that seem to be outside of your control, that seem to happen for no good reason that you can determine. Viktor Frankl was imprisoned in Nazi concentration camps in World War II – it's hard to argue that he was to blame for almost being starved to death. The key point is that he could still choose his response to that situation. He could *decide* whether or not to give up. He chose not to.

It's vital to understand the difference between taking responsibility, and being to blame. We all make mistakes. We make decisions and take actions that end up having negative outcomes – that is an inevitable part of life. When we blame ourselves for the mistake, beating ourselves up, we are dwelling on it – we stay in the past, reliving the mistake over and over. Taking responsibility is about looking forward.

Yes, we acknowledge the mistake, we apologise for it, and work hard to put things right. But we then shift our focus to the future ... to not repeating the same mistake, to doing – and being – better next time round.

Deciding to accept personal responsibility for your life is incredibly liberating. It's also hard. It's the first step on your personal development journey. To realise that when you say "I'm not going for a run today because it's raining" – it's not the weather's fault you didn't go for a run. You chose not to go. Your decision. It's the same when you say "I've got no money because taxes are too high/benefits are too low." That isn't the governments fault. Take a look around – I guarantee that there are people living in the same country as you who are being incredibly successful. The rules are exactly the same for them as they are for you. Is it hard when taxes are high and/or benefits are low? Absolutely it is. But *you always have a choice* about how you respond to that situation.

Your relationships are the same. "My girlfriend is so annoying – she always leaves her stuff lying around." Making that situation better isn't going to be easy, no-one is saying that. Making changes nearly always involves some challenging conversations (Chapter 6 is about Communication, and might help). But those changes won't happen unless *you* take responsibility for them.

I realise some of this sounds pretty harsh, but time and again, you see this same basic principle being written about. Don't just take my word for it:

"It is a painful thing to look at your own trouble and know that you yourself and no one else has made it." Sophocles, Greek playwright, 5th century BCE

"It is not in our stars to hold our destiny, but in ourselves." William Shakespeare, 16th century English author

"There is an expiry date on blaming your parents for steering you in the wrong direction; the moment you are old enough to take the wheel, responsibility lies with you." J.K. Rowling, 21st century British author

LANGUAGE

We've all been around people who whinge and whine all the time, and we know how hard it is not to get dragged down to their level. Being around miserable, pessimistic people brings us down and drains our energy. Now consider the opposite. When we spend time with happy, optimistic people, it rubs off on us. We feel revitalised and full of positive energy. Which do you prefer?!

The idea of having a 'positive mental attitude' is fundamental to our self–education. If we don't believe we can get better, then we won't. It's one of the areas of self–help that can be regarded with (understandable) cynicism, but it doesn't mean walking around with a beatific smile pretending that everything is perfect! Instead, a positive mental attitude is about understanding that we have the power to choose our destination in life.

A crucial element to this is the language that we use. If we are constantly talking about how difficult things are and how many problems we have, then this negativity can become a self-fulfilling prophecy. The issue is that complaining never achieves anything. If we want our situation to get better, we have to take action. If you want to take action, it can help to shift your mindset. Reframe 'problems' as 'opportunities', and think about 'difficulties' as 'challenges'. One of my personal favourites is to replace the word 'hard' with 'tricky'. At first, this can seem like a rather silly technique, but over time changing your language like this can really help. An example of this would be the difference between having a problem with your partner that will be hard to resolve without a difficult conversation. Try changing the language, and instead see it as a challenging situation that requires a tricky conversation, and is an opportunity to make things better. If you can think of it this way you can start to see how you might begin the conversation with a different attitude.

Your attitude towards what life has to offer will be an intrinsic part of how things turn out for you.

It's in your hands – what do you choose?

"When a happy person comes into the room, it is as if another candle has been lit." Ralph Waldo Emerson, 19th century American philosopher

"It is better to light a single candle than to curse the darkness." Origin uncertain

CONCLUSION

"The most precious of all possessions is power over ourselves." John Locke, 17th century English philosopher

The central theme of this book is that we see the same ideas, repeated time and again throughout all of human history. Top of that list is the principle that we can always choose our response, in any given situation.

So, if you do decide to take responsibility, how does this work? Imagine you miss the train to work one morning. Why? Hit snooze once too often? Well, then that's clearly on you. Traffic on the school run a bit worse than you were expecting? Not exactly your fault, but you know it's a possibility so perhaps you should give yourself an extra five minutes tomorrow – and every day after? One of the ticket machines at the station was out of order, so the queues were longer than normal? Well ... that's a bit different. It clearly isn't your fault the machine isn't working – remember we're talking about taking responsibility here, not blaming yourself for every little mishap! And no one is seriously suggesting that every day you need to leave for work early enough to cover the possibility that the traffic is bad, AND there's no parking space, AND a couple of ticket machines are out of order, and so on. (Having said that, if you're the sort of person who consistently makes the train by the skin of their teeth, then maybe you *do* want to think about setting your alarm 15 minutes earlier!). There is a balance to be reached here between not blaming the world for everything that happens to us, and not going too far the other way and blaming ourselves for everything. It's not easy to get that

CHAPTER 2 :: Personal Responsibility

balance, but it starts very simply – with understanding that the choices we make are the thing that has the biggest impact on how our lives turn out.

What about the day when despite your best efforts you arrive on the platform to see your train disappearing into the distance? How do we react? Former US Navy SEAL Jocko Willink has a very simple method for dealing with every challenge that comes his way. When things don't quite work out, he just says, "Good." Missed the train? Good. That means I'll get a seat because the next one isn't usually as busy. And if I get a seat, I can get some work done. It's about your attitude.

As I mentioned earlier – never forget that this goes both ways. We've focused a bit on how you might respond to some of the challenges we all face. What about when good things happen? Well, that works the same. Has one of your kids just had an unforgettably awesome birthday party? Your fault. You put the time and effort in to pay for the hall, organise the games, bake the cake, etc. Be proud of yourself. Just got a promotion in your job? Also your fault. It's because you put the work in to learn the skills needed to level up. You chose to put that effort in, so take a moment to congratulate yourself.

This is such a crucial part of the story. Too many of us are super-quick to beat ourselves up over the bad stuff, but never give ourselves a pat on the back for the good things we do. If you decide to take personal responsibility from here on in then make sure you pay attention to both ends of the spectrum.

Deciding to take personal responsibility isn't easy, but it's worth remembering that there is one enormous upside. As Brené Brown says:

> *"If you own this story you get to write the ending."*

Taking responsibility means that you are in charge. You have control over how your life turns out. This doesn't mean life will be a bed of roses from here on in – there will still be challenges – but reminding yourself that you get to decide the outcome is incredibly exciting.

'The Seven Spiritual Laws of Success' [1994]
Deepak Chopra

SUMMARY: A short guide to fulfilling your potential.
KEY QUOTE: "You can wish for things in the future to be different, but in this moment you have to accept things as they are."

It's got the word 'spiritual' in the title, so no prizes for guessing the style and language contained in this New York Times bestseller! It's a short book, and it differs from some of the other spiritually-inclined books in personal development because each chapter ends with three specific steps – Chopra calls them 'committments' – you can make to start putting each of the laws into practice. The seven laws are:

1. The Law of Pure Potentiality
2. The Law of Giving
3. The Law of 'Karma' or Cause and Effect
4. The Law of Least Effort
5. The Law of Intention and Desire
6. The Law of Detachment
7. The Law of 'Dharma' or Purpose in Life

Some of the language is quite flowery, so it can take time to fully understand the meaning, but it offers a slightly different take on many of the key concepts in self-education.

Chopra makes two points that particularly resonated with me. The first is to remind the reader that taking personal responsibility means not blaming anyone – and that includes yourself. We mustn't blame ourselves for the things that happen, any more than we should blame our parents, teachers, or the traffic warden that gave us a ticket last week. Accept responsibility, make changes if they are needed, but don't beat yourself up.

His second point is a very simple one. He suggests that we should spend our days asking simply: "How can I help?" Sounds like excellent advice to me.

"No one is useless in this world who lightens the burdens of another." Charles Dickens, 19th century English author

MORE LIKE THIS: 'The Monk Who Sold His Ferrari' by Robin Sharma, 'Seasons of Life' by Jim Rohn

CHAPTER 3 :: VALUES

"A man's character is his fate." Heraclitus, Greek philosopher, 5th century BCE

"Search your own heart with all diligence for out of it flow the issues of life." The Bible

WHEN WE THINK OF VALUES, we think of things like honesty, loyalty, trust, and respect. Basic human qualities that all of us consider to be important. These ideas are fundamental principles that we all have to live by – it's not really possible to live an effective life if we disregard them. Think about it: is there a single person you admire that recommends the opposite?

Imagine an individual who doesn't abide by these principles. Someone who is dishonest, disloyal, and untrustworthy, who lies and cheats their way through life. None of us want people like this in our lives. Therefore, unless we want to spend our lives alone, surely none of us should behave like this?

However, like a lot of things in our self-education, taking the action is much more challenging than reading or saying the words. Are we suggesting that everyone has to be a saint, and always hold themselves to the strictest of principles? Well ... no, not really. Firstly, it's probably not possible without becoming some sort of hermit, and secondly, while we might like the idea of keeping strictly to our values at all times, the real world is much more complicated than that! Rarely is a situation black and white – there are always shades of grey involved.

Taking honesty as an example. We can all agree that telling the truth is the right thing to do whenever we can. But consider an ancient Chinese fable that tells the story of a monk standing at a fork in the road. As he waits, a woman runs towards him. She is clearly very distressed, with a black eye and blood running from a cut on her lip. She doesn't say anything, but runs off down the left hand path. A short while later a gang of bandits arrive, and demand that the monk tell them which way the woman went. The monk calmly points to the right hand road, and the thugs head that way.

Now, this is obviously not meant to be a realistic tale – it is a fable – but what does it tell us? It might seem obvious, but this is an example where telling a small lie prevents a greater evil from occurring. The monk deliberately misled the thugs in order to save the woman. But why? What motivated the monk to tell this lie? It was his values. His moral compass led him to make the decision he did.

We all need to do the same – we need to be guided by a moral compass that informs the decisions we make. This applies to the big things in life, like how we treat the secrets people tell us, and whether there is ever a point where breaking that trust is the right choice. If it is just to spread gossip then no, it's clearly not the right thing to do. But if that knowledge can prevent (or perhaps ease) someone else's pain, then there may come a time when betraying that trust for a greater good is the right thing to do – much like the monk in the story.

Your values can also guide some of the smaller decisions in life. Like whether to eat that chocolate cake or not. It may seem odd to frame that decision in terms of your principles – but let's take a deeper look. If your health is something you value highly, then the cake decision looks a bit different. Or perhaps you want to set the right example to your children – what message are you sending them by guzzling another brownie? The flip side of this might be that it's important for you to enjoy life – in which case you could definitely argue that treating yourself to a piece of cake is actually a good thing to do … Clearly this is a very tricky area, and while the fundamental principles might be easy to define, the application of those ideas is much more complex!

The fact that the decisions can get complicated absolutely does not mean we should ignore our values, however. Grab

CHAPTER 3 :: Values

your journal and write a list of all the values that mean something to you. There are no right or wrong answers, so think broadly at this point. The next step is to narrow the list down to the 3–5 values that are most important to you. The goal is to end up with a list where removing one of the values feels like it would be too much of a compromise.

No-one can tell you what your values should be, and how you should prioritise the different areas of your life. It is different for all of us. For that reason, I'm afraid this chapter doesn't contain much in the way of practical advice. Instead, it is an introduction to a variety of different concepts. Hopefully some of them will resonate with you, and help you figure out the areas that are most important to you personally.

"The most important knowledge is that which guides the way you lead your life." Seneca, Roman philosopher, 1st century

"Integrity is doing the right thing, even when no one is looking." CS Lewis, British author, 20th century

THE GOLDEN RULE

"That which you hate to be done to you, do not do to another." Ancient Egyptian papyrus, c.7th–4th century BCE

"Why does one hurt others knowing what it is to be hurt?" Ancient Tamil tradition, India, date uncertain

"Whatever is disagreeable to yourself, do not do unto others." Pahlavi Texts, Ancient Persia, date uncertain

The concept of the Golden Rule is a part of every major belief and ethics system that we know of. It is a central principle of Buddhism, Christianity, Confucianism, Islam, Hinduism and Taoism, to name but a few. It is in texts from the ancient Babylonians, the Mayans, the Chinese and the Native Americans. There has to be a reason that people from all eras and all corners of the globe have agreed that treating other people fairly is fundamental to living a good life. The reason is simple: it's the right thing to do – and deep down, we all know that.

In its broadest interpretation, the Golden Rule encompasses how we behave towards ourselves, other people, and the world around us. It covers everything from the self-talk that goes on in our heads (see P95), to whether we smile at the person serving us coffee, to whether or not we put our empty cup in the bin, or just drop it on the pavement once we're finished with it. Essentially, we should all lead by example. It is generally more reliable to judge a person by their actions rather than their words – so remember that for every action you take, someone is watching you ... and – most likely – judging you.

Living this way isn't easy. We all have those days where even being polite to the shop assistant is hard. But like so many other things in life, we can get in the habit of following the Golden Rule. Don't beat yourself up every time you 'break' the Rule – be aware, take responsibility, and decide to do better next time. And when next time you are better – don't forget to give yourself a little pat on the back. Celebrate your wins, however small they might be.

THE GOLDEN MEAN

The Golden Mean is usually attributed to Aristotle. There is some debate about it's exact origins, but it's definitely been around for thousands of years which is the important point from our perspective. The Golden Mean states that the best path usually lies between two extremes. An example would be that courage is the path lying between the two extremes of recklessness at one end and cowardice at the other. As well as Aristotle and the Greeks, both the Buddha and Confucius use the same concept. Note that we again have the same idea developing in three distinct parts of the world at approximately the same time ...

It's an idea that can be applied to almost anything. In relationships, no-one should be a doormat, and neither should one person get their own way all the time. The best path lies between these two extremes – sometimes standing up for yourself, and at other times being prepared to compromise. Financially, the Golden Mean is about having enough that we can provide a decent life for ourselves and our loved ones, but not so much that we end up living an excessive, wasteful life. There will always be room for debate over precisely what 'a decent life' means, of course, and it will mean different things to different people. Perhaps one person feels that holidays are unnecessary, while another might think that two or three holidays a year is not particularly excessive. There is no right or wrong answer here – what is important is that you understand what your priorities are, and what balance means to you. Understand also that your opinions will probably change over time as you learn more. One of my favourite quotes is from British philosopher Alain de Botton, who said:

> *"Anyone who isn't embarrassed of who they were last year probably isn't learning enough."*

Using the Golden Mean doesn't stop you from setting big goals – you definitely should. If you want that dream home, or you want to set up a non–profit organisation that educates thousands of kids in Africa (or both!), then go for it. But as you progress on your journey, remember that it's generally a good idea to try and avoid the extremes.

DEFINING SUCCESS

Who do you think of when you hear the word 'successful'? And why?

Have you ever really stopped to consider what success means to you? Does it mean getting on the front page of a magazine, having 100,000 followers on Instagram, driving a Ferrari … or is it something more than that?

Before you can determine whether you are successful or not, you need to know what success means to you. You need to clearly define 'success'. What are your priorities? You might be quite money–orientated – that's great – but where do you draw the line? What is 'enough' to you? And what price are you prepared to pay in other ways? How much time are you willing to sacrifice? Is that too much? Do your relationships suffer because you work long hours? Does working 12 hours a day mean your life is empty in other areas? There are no right and wrong answers – it will be different for everybody. But each of us needs to understand what success means for us personally.

Ultimately, it comes down to balance. There are a couple of different ways to think about this. Stephen Covey says that in order to be satisfied we need four things:

1. To live (be healthy, be able to do the things we enjoy)

2. To learn (be fulfilled in our work and social lives)

3. To love (have deep relationships with our family and friends)

4. To leave a legacy (be involved in something that has meaning and purpose)

Another way to look at it divides life into slightly more specific categories – Google 'wheel of life' for some examples. The exact words and descriptions may vary, but they usually contain some or all of the following:

- Physical health
- Mental stimulation
- Spiritual wellbeing
- Family and Friends
- Work and Money
- Fun and Adventure
- Contribution

Find a set of categories that works for you, and then spend some time writing down what 'success' in each of those areas would look like for you personally. It's important here that you don't use your definition of success as an excuse to

CHAPTER 3 :: Values

stop you achieving things. An easy way out of making hard decisions is to pretend you never wanted it in the first place. If success for you includes a Ferrari, don't pretend it doesn't by convincing yourself that it's just a car, and material things shouldn't really mean anything to you.

The idea of clearly defining what something means to you can be applied to a lot of other ideas besides success. It's worth thinking about what things like happiness, good health and contribution really mean to you. It will help you make better decisions, and the consequence of better decisions is a more fulfilling life.

PRIORITIES

"Things which matter most must never be at the mercy of things that matter least." Johann Wolfgang von Goethe, 18th century German author

Having a clear understanding of what is important to you is a crucial step towards becoming more productive. For example, if you know that 'Contribution' is more important to you than 'Fun and Adventure', then the decision about whether to attend the PTA meeting or head out on your mountain bike becomes a little easier to make.

Understand that whenever you say "I don't have time for this" what you are really saying is "This isn't a priority for me". We always manage to find time for the things we think are important. Realise that when you sit down to watch your favourite TV show, what you are saying is "This is the most important thing for me to be doing right now." This is not necessarily a bad thing – it's important to relax and unwind – but be honest with yourself about what else you could be doing with that time.

We'll go into this in more detail in Chapter 5 when we talk about Taking Action, but for now remember that whatever you choose to do, you are always saying 'no' to something else. Make sure you're saying 'no' to the right things.

MISSION STATEMENT

OK ... here's one of those much maligned self-development phrases that might be making you shudder! Simply put, a Mission Statement is an expression of the values that are important to you personally, which helps prioritise your daily decisions.

To start creating your mission statement, as you go through life gather together the ideas and quotes that strike you as being fundamentally important. As you gather more information, you'll start to see themes emerging. The ideas will get clearer in your head, and you will find yourself consciously referring back to them when making decisions. Eventually, you will be able to actually write out your personal mission statement – but don't worry if you can't quite articulate it yet. The value is as much to do with the process of creation – of taking the time to really think about what is most important to you. It's like doing a piece of art. You start with a blank page and some basic colours. You start sketching, gradually adding more detail, and as you work the picture gets clearer. Going back to your mission statement, you may find that you can articulate everything that is important to you in a sentence or two, but for most people it will be a bit longer than that. You don't want a page long statement though: remember that this is an expression of your values that you can refer to when you are struggling with a decision. If it's too detailed, it will probably just confuse you more!

Mission statements are fantastically useful on a personal level, and you may find you can use them in other areas of your life – family and business being the most obvious examples. If you do start using them with groups of people, it is crucial that everyone is involved in the process. A family mission statement will not work if Mum comes up with it, and tries to impose it on everyone else in the home. For a mission statement to be successful, everyone has to buy into it, and that will only happen if they contribute to its creation.

This is why company mission statements are so often such a disaster — they are decided upon by a small group of executives who are out of touch with what is actually going on in the business.

Forming a mission statement takes time and effort — but done well, they can be a fantastically useful tool.

> **'Seth's Blog'**
> *Seth Godin*
> SUMMARY: Short snippets of value-driven advice.
> KEY QUOTE: "People like us do things like this".
>
> Seth Godin is best known as a marketing guru (one of the few people who actually deserves that title). Following a successful business career, he now publishes books, a podcast and a daily blog which he uses to teach his fundamental message of "people like us do things like this". What he means is that the way you conduct yourself — both in business and in life — will determine the sort of people who are attracted to you. If you do business ethically and responsibly, then you will have customers who believe that is important. But if you cut corners and try to rip people off, then you only have yourself to blame for the sort of people who will use your services. This is a brilliant insight into how to do business the right way, but the idea is applicable in every aspect of life.
>
> If you're primarily interested in a new perspective on doing business in the 21st century, his books are excellent. Each one covers a specific topic, and Godin always gets straight to the point. 'Tribes' is an excellent place to start, with great lessons and observations on Leadership. His podcast is called 'Akimbo' and is always thought-provoking, but for the broadest overview of his ideas and how to apply them, visit his blog. It's one of the most popular in the world, and each day Godin publishes a short piece of

advice that usually only takes a couple of minutes to read. Although they are ostensibly about business, Godin has such strong values underpinning his ideas that his blog posts become excellent advice for life in general, not just business. If you only ever sign up for one newsletter, make it Godin's.

"I've learned that people will forget what you said, people will forget what you did, but they will never forget how you made them feel." Maya Angelou, 20th century American writer

MORE LIKE THIS: 'Do/ Purpose' by David Hieatt, 'Let My People Go Surfing' by Yvon Chouinard

WHAT ABOUT MONEY?

"To acquire money requires valour, to keep money requires prudence, and to spend money well is an art." Berthold Auerbach, 19th century German author

"Money is a terrible master but an excellent servant." PT Barnum, 19th century American businessman

For me, understanding how to value money, and where to place it in my list of priorities was one of the hardest parts of the journey – and I'm still not sure I've got the balance quite right.

We talked earlier about the Golden Mean, and it now forms the basis of my thoughts about money. In the past, I have had times of relative affluence, and quickly fell into bad habits of overspending and developing an unhealthy desire for 'more'. It didn't make me happy. I've also had times when money has been really tight, and I was pretty miserable then, too!

Seth Godin says "you can tell yourself any story you want about money, and it's better to tell yourself a story that you can happily live with." When people have a lot of money, it's easy for them to fall into the habit of thinking that they couldn't possibly survive without a new car every couple of years, or freshly ground coffee every morning. That clearly isn't true. No one is saying we should all live like hermits, and there's nothing wrong with having nice things.

Of course, this works at the other end of the spectrum. Many people who are surviving by the skin of their teeth manage to convince themselves that they don't actually want more money. They take the moral high ground, and their story is that money doesn't make you happy, so why bother trying to get more of it? Again, this is not a story that will serve you particularly well. It is undoubtedly true that money doesn't buy you happiness, but it can definitely help take some of the stress away, allowing you time to focus on other more important things.

Whatever story you tell yourself about money, make sure that it is yours, and not one you have just borrowed from your parents, friends or work colleagues. (This happens in other areas too, of course, but it is particularly prevalent with people's attitudes to money).

The other side to having more money centres around what you decide to do with your extra income. Once the basic needs of you and your loved ones are met, you have a series of decisions to make. Having more money than you need doesn't necessarily mean going on another holiday or upgrading your car more often. One of the few cliches I have an issue with is 'money is the root of all evil'. It has been slightly corrupted from the original, which said that it is *love* of money, or the *pursuit* of money above all other things which cause the problems. Money itself is just an object – like a car. The car itself is not bad, but at the hands of an irresponsible driver it can cause great harm. Money is the same – it's not the cash itself that leads to problems, it's how people choose to use the money that is the issue. When rich people do bad things, there is a tendency to somehow blame the money. And when poor people do bad things, you will often find that blamed on their lack of money. No. Whether rich or poor, it is *people* who make decisions – and we all need to take personal responsibility for the choices we make.

I'm not saying this is easy. For example, very few people truly 'need' a car worth more than about £10,000 (and you could probably argue for a much lower figure than that) ... but it's OK to 'want' a more expensive car. Just don't kid yourself about the reasons you bought that £25,000 car – about the story you are telling yourself.

Ultimately, the only person who can decide what is an appropriate amount to spend on a car – or anything other material item – is you. And it's really important that you don't feel guilty about it, whether you spent £500 ("Oh, but maybe I should get a bike, because it's better for the environment...") or £50,000 ("I really like my leather seats and heads–up display, but would it be better to be investing that money rather than spending it?").

The point of all this is that we need to remember that money is a tool, capable of both doing good and causing harm, depending on how we decide to use it. Wherever you currently fall on the wealth spectrum, give some serious thought to why you're there and how you really feel about your situation. Take responsibility for that, decide if you want to change it, then go take some action.

> **'Richest Man in Babylon' [1926]**
> *George S. Clason*
> SUMMARY: A short fable, packed with sound advice on how to manage money more effectively.
> KEY QUOTE: "Wealth, like a tree, grows from a tiny seed."
>
> This was the first personal development book I read – and it almost put me off for life! Written in 1926 in the style of an old fable, it's full of sentences like "Gold, indeed, clingeth to the cautious owner, even as it flees the careless owner", which isn't going to be to everyone's taste – however good the advice may be! Leaving the style to one side, the information it contains about how we should handle our money is still incredibly relevant. There are two main lessons:

1. "A part of all you earn is yours to keep." No matter how much or how little you earn, save the first 10%. If you can save more than this, great – but you should never save less. If that means spending less on clothes, or your TV package, then that's what you need to do. If you never save, you can never get ahead, and the sooner you start saving, the more powerful your savings become as they accumulate over time. (If you're not familiar with the power of the Compound Effect, then Google it now). The next money you earn, before you do anything else – put at least 10% into a savings account. You'll be surprised how quickly it builds up, and how this starts to change your perspective on money generally.

2. "Better a little caution than a great regret." Be smart with your savings. Invest in things you understand, and with people you trust. If you don't understand cryptocurrency, you shouldn't be risking your money there. When you don't fully understand the risks, you're basically gambling ... and in gambling, the house always wins in the long run.

There is also an overriding personal development philosophy that runs through the book:

"The more of wisdom we know, the more we may earn."

This applies to both of the main lessons. Learn a little about how to invest your money – even if it's just to compare the interest rates on different bank accounts so you get the best rate, rather than just using the same bank as your parents. You don't need to be an expert, but don't start dabbling in stocks and shares (for example) without some basic knowledge.

This philosophy of learning can also be applied to how much you earn. Why should your boss give you a pay rise, just for doing your job the same as you did last year? If you want to increase your income, you need to learn new skills – you need to get better at your job. Once you're better than the person next to you, then you deserve to earn more. And the brilliant thing is, this is in your hands. With online resources like Udemy, CreativeLive and TED, and the wealth of books and audio that is available, we can all improve our skills for a very minimal financial outlay – and often for free! Hold back on that Chinese takeaway this week, and invest in yourself instead.

The more you learn, the more you earn.

"Too many people spend money they haven't earned, to buy things they don't want, to impress people that they don't like." Will Rogers, 20th century American actor

MORE LIKE THIS: 'Rich Dad, Poor Dad' by Robert Kiyosaki, 'The 4-Hour Work Week' by Tim Ferriss

'Doing Good Better' [2015]
William Macaskill

SUMMARY: A detailed look at the best ways to make a difference.

KEY QUOTE: "When it comes to helping others, being unreflective often means being ineffective."

If the idea of giving some of your money to charity is important to you, then you may find reading this book helps you evaluate the best way to do so. Macaskill is an advocate of 'effective altruism', arguing that we should take a more questioning and analytical approach to our giving. He suggests we take as much time thinking about how we spend the money we give to charity as we do when considering a new washing machine, for example.

He offers ways to assess the real impact that an organisation has, and offers numerous ideas for how each of us can have the most impact. Even if you only allocate a few pounds a year to giving, Macaskill says that every penny can either disappear into a vague pot where it doesn't really make a difference, or it can be used to have a definite impact.

It's a very thought-provoking book, taking a long overdue look at traditional giving methods and offering practical improvements that each of us can easily implement.

"Do what you can, with what you've got, where you are."
Bill Widener, quoted by American President Theodore Roosevelt in his autobiography, 20th century

MORE LIKE THIS: 'The Blue Sweater' by Jacqueline Novogratz, 'Start Something That Matters' by Blake Mycoskie

CHAPTER 4 :: GOAL SETTING

GOAL SETTING

"Man is a goal seeking animal. His life only has meaning if he is reaching out and striving for his goals." Aristotle, Greek philosopher, 4th century BCE

IT WASN'T THAT LONG AGO that I had never formally 'set a goal' for myself, and when I initially came across the idea I was quite resistant to it. I couldn't see the point in taking time to set goals – I thought my time was better spent getting on with things. Then one day, somebody pointed out to me that we all set goals, it's just a question of how big they are. Most of us actually set several goals every day – get the kids to school by 8.30, get to work by 8.50, get to the post office in your lunch break, get the kids to bed before your favourite soap or the football starts, and so on. We usually hit these targets fairly regularly. We then have slightly longer term goals – perhaps to go on holiday next summer, or to get a new car this year … quite often we are less successful with these sorts of goals. We'll look at some possible reasons why – as well as some tactics to change that – in a short while, but first lets talk about why we should set goals in the first place.

Imagine you have a long journey to go on – you're flying to New York, and you have to be there by 8pm next Tuesday. It's pretty obvious that the most effective way of arriving on time is to work backwards. You book a flight that gets you there in time – probably arriving earlier than necessary, just to be on the safe side. Then you work out the best way to get to the airport. Do you drive, and park your car? Perhaps it's simpler to get a train or a taxi? How long does each option take? What's the most cost effective option? Once that is decided, you know what time you need to leave your house. Next you decide how much to take, and how long it will take to pack … and so on. You get the idea. By working back in this way, you eventually work out what needs to be done, and what time it needs to be done by. Planning like this minimises stress, and maximises your chances of success.

Now imagine the alternative ... You have to be in New York by 8pm next Tuesday. A friend told you the flight takes about 6 hours, so next Tuesday you arrive at your nearest airport around midday. What do you think your chances of making your appointment are? Pretty slim, right? Of course, you might get lucky – perhaps your friend was right about it taking 6 hours, and there happens to be a flight leaving at 1pm that has a space on it. Happy days! But I doubt many of us would treat our trip to New York that casually.

Think about how you plan your life. Is it full of vague ideas about getting a new car later this year, or taking a month to explore India at some undefined point in the future? Or do you know exactly what car you want, how much it costs, and therefore how much you need to save each month?

Maybe it's time to start planning these things a bit more seriously?

GOALS V DREAMS

"A goal is a dream with a deadline." Napoleon Hill, 20th century American author

There is a huge difference between dreams and goals. Dreams are brilliant – we should all have them. As kids, we did – I grew up wanting to be an astronaut, wrestler and racing car driver, and firmly believed I could do all three at the same time! Pretty standard stuff for an eight year old boy. But somewhere along the line, those dreams all got knocked out of me. The same thing happens to almost all of us – we lose our ability to dream, we get told to stop being silly, to be more realistic. This usually comes from people who really care about us, and are honestly trying to help. But losing our ability to dream big is actually really important. If we want to change our lives, it starts with thinking bigger.

So, grab your journal and spend the next 5–10 minutes

writing out a list of your dreams ... the ones you had as a kid ... the ones you have now, but that sound too far-fetched, so you've never told anyone about them ... get them all out of your head and onto the page ... It doesn't matter how ridiculous they sound – we're not looking for practical at the moment. If you've always dreamed of walking on Mars, then write it down. Stop reading, and start writing.

> **'The Magic of Thinking Big' [1959]**
> *David Schwartz*
> SUMMARY: Motivational, easy to read; great when you need a pick-me-up.
> KEY QUOTE: "Action cures fear."
>
> A decade ago, the idea that I would be recommending this book to other people would have seemed impossible. It's got a very 'rah-rah' tone that won't be for everyone – as an example, Chapter 2 of the book is called 'Cure Yourself of Excusitis, the Failure Disease'. It goes on to list the four main excuses people give as to why things aren't working out for them, and – importantly – also gives solid, practical advice for how to combat these excuses.
>
> The 13 chapters cover the main personal development areas, from 'Get the Action Habit' to 'Use Goals to Help You Grow', and everything in between. Whatever the subject, Schwartz's positivity and enthusiasm comes through on every page. It's also an easier read than something like 'Think and Grow Rich' or '7 Habits', making this a good stepping-stone to some of the more detailed and in-depth material out there.
>
> *"Every great dream begins with a dreamer. Always remember, you have within you the strength, the patience, and the passion to reach for the stars to change the world."*
> *Harriet Tubman, 19th century American activist*
>
> MORE LIKE THIS: 'The Power of Positive Thinking'

by Norman Vincent Peale, 'Feel the Fear and Do It Anyway' by Susan Jeffers

HAVING SMART GOALS

Once you've got your list of dreams, it's time to start turning them into goals – things we can actually achieve by taking small steps forward, day after day. A really good way to do this is to set SMART goals. This technique was first mentioned by George T. Doran in 1981, and there have since been numerous variations on his basic idea. SMART is an acronym, and you will find some variation on what the letters stand for. The most effective system I've found has the letters standing for:

- **S**PECIFIC
- **M**OTIVATING
- **A**CHIEVABLE
- **R**ELEVANT
- **T**RACKABLE

An effective goal needs to be all of these things, and it's not a complicated process.

SPECIFIC: "I want to go on holiday this year" is a dream. It's vague, and – frankly – it's not likely to happen. "I want to stay at the Sunset Hotel in the Seychelles for two weeks next April" is a goal. It's specific – the parameters are set, so you know what you're dealing with, and what action you're going to need to take. If you want to move house, what area do you want to move to? How many bedrooms do you want? How big is the garden? And so on. Be SPECIFIC about what you're working towards.

MOTIVATING: How badly do you want it? This is probably the most important element. A goal has to be something you want to do, and the bigger the goal, the more you need to want it. When pursuing the goal gets

CHAPTER 4 :: Goal Setting

challenging – and it will – you need a powerful reason to keep going. If you want to watch the Olympic 100m Final on the TV, that's one thing – it needs some planning, but it's pretty easy. However, if you want to watch the race live at the stadium then that's going to involve a different level of commitment, so you're going to need to be a lot more motivated. If that's long been a dream of yours, then that could be exactly the motivation you need. On the other hand, if you have zero interest in sports then the 100m final won't motivate you, so you're unlikely to succeed. It's really important to note the role other people can play in your motivation. Maybe the Olympics don't interest you, but perhaps your Mum loves them ... if that's the case then that 100m Final could still be a goal, but it becomes about the person, rather than the event itself. Whichever way you approach it, your goals have to MOTIVATE you to put the work in.

ACHIEVABLE: Setting big goals is a good thing, but you have to be realistic about it. If you want to be a millionaire, then that's great – but if you currently earn £20,000 a year, then setting a target to be a millionaire within a year is extremely unlikely to happen. Set goals that challenge you, that take you out of your comfort zone, but try to strike a balance between pushing yourself and not setting ridiculous targets that will just frustrate you. An important thing to note here is that dates can be adjusted. Particularly with long-term goals, it can be hard to predict exactly how things are going to go. Life throws curveballs at us all from time to time, so don't beat yourself up if you have to adjust a date slightly ... And remember that this can also work the other way – sometimes things go better than expected, and you can actually bring a date forward! One thing to note here: most of us overestimate what we can do in one year, but radically underestimate what can be accomplished in ten years ... Challenge yourself to see what you can ACHIEVE.

RELEVANT: It's important that you work on goals that are relevant to your current life and situation. Perhaps you've always wanted to spend three months backpacking around South–East Asia. That's great! But if you've got a couple of kids at school, then this might be something that has to go on the back–burner for a while. Relevance is about striking a balance between goals that really motivate you, but that are also practical. Having said that – don't use this as an excuse for putting things off. If you want to backpack for three months, is there a way you can do it with your kids? Imagine how much more fun that would be! Don't immediately dismiss the big, audacious goals – but make sure they are RELEVANT to your life … and to the life you want to lead.

TRACKABLE: You need to be able to monitor your progress. If you can measure something, you can improve it. Being specific in your goals will really help here. Saying "I want to lose weight" is hard to track. But if you say "I want to lose 5kg by June 1st", then you will know exactly how you're doing. Making it trackable also helps you avoid setting goals where success might be hard to measure. "I want a more meaningful relationship with my partner" is not really specific, or trackable – how do you measure "meaningful"? Making improvements in these kinds of areas is obviously incredibly important, but you have to make sure you can monitor your progress. Maybe a better way to improve a relationship is to set the goal of having a phone–free, sit–down lunch with your partner once a week? That would certainly help make your relationship more meaningful, and those lunches are something you can easily TRACK.

Let's look at a specific example, and see how we might go about it. Let's say you've always wanted to go to the Seychelles, so you spend some time researching it. The best time to go is April, and the Sunset Hotel ticks all the boxes. Imagine it's now February. Looking at the prices you can't afford to go this year, but that information gives you an idea of how much you need to save every month. This goal is now

Specific, Motivating and Achievable. It's also Relevant as you can afford to take the whole family and it will provide you all with memories that will last a lifetime. Lastly, it's Trackable because you can have a separate holiday account that the money goes in to each month. All you need to do now is set another goal for the GoPro you want to take!

Pick one of the dreams that you wrote in your journal a few minutes ago, and turn it into a goal using this system:

- Make it SPECIFIC – dates, times, location and other details
- Write down why it MOTIVATES you
- Be realistic about the commitment needed to ACHIEVE the goal
- Make sure it's RELEVANT to your life now, and the life you want
- Work out how to TRACK your progress, so you'll know when it's completed

It's really important to write your goals down, and refer to them daily. Spend a few moments every morning reminding yourself what you want, how you're going to get it, and – most importantly – why you want it.

Really big goals might need to be broken down into smaller steps. One step towards that dream house might be to increase your income over the next five years. And before you can make more money, you might need to get some specialised training. Keep breaking it down until you find your starting point.

Bear in mind that while the SMART goals system is an excellent way to get clear in your head about what you want, it isn't actually doing anything. For you to attain your goals, you're also going to need to put the work in. Whether things are going well or you're getting a bit behind, be realistic with yourself about why that is happening. Move deadlines and be prepared to adjust course if necessary – but never stop working.

"When it is obvious that the goals cannot be reached, don't adjust the goals, adjust the action steps." Confucius, Chinese philosopher, 6th century BCE

Fear Setting
Tim Ferriss

SUMMARY: A powerful system for tackling big goals.
KEY QUOTE: "Conquering fear = defining fear."

Often we can find ways to talk ourselves out of setting the really massive goals. There are lots of reasons for this, but most often it is because we are scared. The voices in our heads are telling us we don't deserve that new car, or we're not good enough to get promoted – "who the hell do you think you are?!" These voices can be vicious. We talk to ourselves in a way that we wouldn't dream of talking to any other human being.

We go into this in more detail in Chapter 6, but for now understand that almost everybody suffers with negative self-talk – even the unbelievably successful people we all admire, they are dealing with the exact same issues as the rest of us. They are their own worst enemy! Thankfully, they've also found ways to deal with these issues. From what I've learned, it seems the voices never entirely go away, but there are things we can do to lessen the impact of the negative voices in our heads. One of these is by using a process called 'Fear Setting'.

This is a thought exercise from Tim Ferriss that I first came across in his TED talk, and that he repeats in his brilliant book 'Tools of Titans' (See P141). It is widely accepted that the biggest barrier for most people is fear – whether that is asking someone on a date, changing jobs, starting that difficult conversation with a loved one ... whatever the challenge, it's nearly always fear that holds us back.

CHAPTER 4 :: Goal Setting

Ferriss suggests confronting that fear directly by putting it down on a piece of paper, digging in to what it really means, and thinking about what the actual consequences might be. You need to get the details from the book or TED talk, but the basic process is:

1. Start by asking yourself: "What if I ... quit my job/ask that person out/start that conversation/ etc?"
2. Write a list of the 10–20 worst things that could happen. For each one, put next to it how you might prevent that thing from happening, and also how you might fix the situation if it ever does happens.
3. List the benefits of an attempt, or even partial success. Give this a mark out of ten.
4. List the costs of inaction – physically, financially, emotionally, etc. Give this a mark out of ten as well.

You then compare the two scores you've got – potential benefits vs potential costs. This is a really tangible way to assess the situation – if the upside is only a five, and the risks are a seven, well ... maybe it's not such a good idea after all. But what you'll find happens surprisingly often is that you are risking a score of 3–4 of pain for a potential 8–9 of positive impact.

The process takes 20–30 minutes to do properly, so it's not something you use on a daily basis. But when it comes to those big decisions, you might find this really helps to understand the reality of the situation ... make sure it's not just fear holding you back in life.

"Nothing in life is to be feared, it is only to be understood. Now is the time to understand more, so that we may fear less." Marie Curie, 20th century Polish–French scientist

Goal Setting v Processes
Scott Adams

SUMMARY: An alternative way of thinking about goals.

KEY QUOTE: "Every skill you acquire doubles your odds of success."

Goal Setting can feel like a strange thing to do, and a system like SMART goals won't work for everyone. Another technique that you might find useful is outlined by Scott Adams (creator of the 'Dilbert' comic strip) in his book 'How to Fail at Almost Everything and Still Win Big'. He reframes his long term goals in terms of 'processes' he wants to go through along the way so that even if the specific goal isn't quite achieved, the effort is still worthwhile.

It's important to note that he defines 'processes' very broadly – it might be acquiring a new skill, like learning a language, or getting better at tennis, but it could also be developing a relationship with someone new, or becoming happier. The crucial point is that you provide yourself with a clear benefit outside of the specific goal itself.

In practical terms, what that means is that in addition (or even as an alternative) to setting yourself the goal of losing 6kgs in the next three months, you also think about the skills you might acquire along the way. In order to lose weight, you need to change both your eating and your training habits. So perhaps you could decide to learn about the Slow Carb diet to help you eat more healthily, and to also improve your running technique to minimise the risk of injury while you train. If you improve your skills in those two areas, you'll almost certainly lose the weight – and even if you don't quite hit that 6kg target, you will have improved your knowledge and understanding in two really important areas.

Going back to our imaginary holiday to the

CHAPTER 4 :: Goal Setting

Seychelles ... In order to get to the Sunset Hotel you're probably going to need to save some money, so one of the skills you could improve might be money management. It's an opportunity to get better at planning your weekly or monthly budget, enabling you to save enough for the holiday. Perhaps you could also learn a bit about investing in order to make your money work for you rather than the other way round.

This concept can work in reverse. If there's a skill you've always wanted to learn but never quite got round to, perhaps you can set yourself a practical target that incorporates that skill. Always wanted to take up painting? Maybe set yourself the goal of sending personalised Christmas cards this year, featuring a piece of your art on the front. If you've always wanted to learn Spanish, make that next holiday somewhere you can actually use those skills!

Separating (or linking) goals and 'processes' in this way can make the tasks at hand seem more exciting, worthwhile and achievable. Go back to your goal list, and see how many skills you could develop along the way.

"Man's mind, once stretched by a new idea, never regains its original dimensions." Oliver Wendell Holmes Sr, 19th century American polymath

Brian Tracy

Tracy is one of the venerable grandfathers of self development, speaking all over the world, authoring 50+ books, and working as a trainer and consultant for some of the biggest companies in the world. I'm going to cover two of his books here that link this chapter to the next, and that both start with the same sentence:

"This is a wonderful time to be alive."

'Goals!' [2010]

SUMMARY: A clear, comprehensive and easy-to-follow guide to achieving your goals.

KEY QUOTE: "Write down your goals, make plans to achieve them, and work on your plans every single day."

The 21 chapters in this book are all fairly short – usually 10–15 pages (or one day's worth of reading). They are packed full of brilliant advice, and each one ends with a list of questions to answer. Treat this almost like a 'work book', and even if you've never set a goal in your life before, by the time you've finished reading you'll feel like a goal-setting ninja! Tracy's style is gently persuasive, optimistic, but with a healthy dose of reality.

The subtitle of this book is 'How to get everything you want – faster than you ever thought possible', and Tracy provides an excellent framework for you to do just that.

"It always seems impossible until it is done." Nelson Mandela, 20th century South African leader

MORE LIKE THIS: 'Getting Things Done' by David Allen, 'The One Thing' by Gary Keller with Jay Papasan

'Eat That Frog!' [2001]

SUMMARY: Short, simple read about getting the important things done.

KEY QUOTE: "An average person who develops the

habit of setting clear priorities and getting important tasks completed quickly runs rings around a genius who talks a lot and makes wonderful plans but who gets very little done."

This little book specifically deals with procrastination, and offers very specific advice and techniques on how to battle it. The essential message is to make the worst task of the day the first thing that you do. If you know you've got to eat a frog at some point today – what's the point in putting it off until later? You might as well get it over and done with so you can enjoy the rest of the day, instead of having the job constantly niggling at the back of your mind … As Tracy says:

"The first rule of frog eating is this: If you have to eat frogs, eat the ugliest one first … Second rule of frog eating: If you have to eat a live frog at all, it doesn't pay to sit and look at it for very long."

Tracy acknowledges that this – like many things – is "easy to do; easy not to do", and one of the things I like about him is how many techniques and tactics he provides. Tracy starts by advising us to 'Set the Table' (i.e. set goals), then progresses through (among other things) 'Focus on the key result areas', 'Slice and dice the task' and 'Single handle every task'.

It's a short, easy to read book that packs a real punch in terms of the quality of information it contains. If procrastination is something you struggle with (and let's be honest, who doesn't?!), then you'll get huge value from learning how to 'Eat That Frog!'

"It is easier to resist at the beginning than at the end."
Leonardo da Vinci, 15th century Italian polymath

MORE LIKE THIS: 'The War of Art' by Steven Pressfield, 'Show Your Work' by Austin Kleon

CHAPTER 5 :: TAKE ACTION

WHAT IS PROCRASTINATION ?

"I wasted time, and now doth time waste me." Shakespeare, 16th century English author

"You may delay, but time will not." Benjamin Franklin, 18th century American polymath

"Inaction breeds doubt and fear. Action breeds confidence and courage. If you want to conquer fear, do not sit home and think about it. Go out and get busy." Dale Carnegie, 20th century American author

PROCRASTINATION MEANS PUTTING THINGS OFF until later. Sometimes it's small things, like doing the washing up. Sometimes it's really big things, like having that tough conversation with your partner. It's something we all do, even though we know we shouldn't. The really terrible thing is that we know putting things off only makes it worse, leading to feelings of guilt and inadequacy. We end up feeling really bad about ourselves … but we find a flimsy excuse, and put it off anyway.

The good news is that overcoming procrastination is a skill like any other – you can work on it. Practice being productive, and eventually that will become your default habit. With the right mindset and work ethic, you can teach yourself to minimise the amount of procrastination you do by establishing new habits and routines that enable you to GSD. Get Stuff Done. (Or Get S*** Done, depending on your preference).

We can get better at this, but it's not quite as simple as writing a 'To Do' list and then ticking jobs off. To begin, we need to be doing the tasks that are going to make a real difference to our lives. We also need to make sure the list needs to match with our values. How do we do this?

Firstly, we need to be clear on our personal values – what are the most important things to you? As the months and years go by this will evolve, and that's OK. Use your values as they currently stand, then write a list of all the things you need to get done. Put it down on a piece of paper – everything from attending the school play, to the vacuuming, to that work deadline that is looming. Next, realise that writing the list is actually you procrastinating (my fault – I asked you to write the list. I apologise) … while writing the list, you aren't actually getting anything done. This is really important – writing lists is *not* GSD!

OK. You've got a list. Some of it will seem very mundane. 'Do the washing', for instance. Initially it might be hard to see how these things match up with your values … but if the health and wellbeing of you and your loved ones is important to you, then maybe 'doing the washing' starts looking a bit different. Spending your day in dirty clothes isn't great for anyone's physical health or mental wellbeing. Doing the washing is never likely to get more interesting, but reframing a boring job in this way might help you GSD.

Now you need to work out what order to do things. For that, you need a system – something that you can repeat – something that can become a habit. The following method combines ideas from Warren Buffet (an American investor and one of the wealthiest people in the world), Ivy Lee (a business advisor regarded as the founder of modern public relations), and everyone who has ever said "put first things first". This is what you do:

1. Write down all the things you want to get done.

2. Write a new list with the top five tasks ranked in order of importance. This is List A.

3. What is left becomes List B.

4. Get to work on the most important task on List A. Do nothing else until this task is completed.

5. Work through the rest of List A.

6. When all the jobs on List A are complete, start the process again.

CHAPTER 5 :: Take Action

Here's the really important bit. Think of List B as your 'NOT to-do list'. You avoid those tasks at all costs – they are now distractions. You do your utmost to avoid List B until List A is complete. Focusing on List A forces your attention on a handful of your most important tasks. You end up with five completed projects instead of 20 half-completed ones. Even if you only get the first item on List A done, your day has still been effective – you got the most important job of the day done.

If that system seems a bit long-winded, a simpler version of it is to set 'Today's Top Three'. Imagine you could only do three things today. If that was the case, which three are the most important? Jot them down, then get started on the first one.

Whatever system you use, it's best to get started on the first task as early in the day as you can. That way you get the rest of the day to enjoy the sense of satisfaction at having nailed your most important task, rather than spending hours living with that nagging sense that you've still got something to do. In practice, you can't always be as ruthless as I'm making it sound. For example, you may reach a point where you need someone else's input to complete a task and you need to wait for them. Or perhaps there's a time constraint – if the most important job is making the time to go for lunch with your partner at 1pm, and it's only 10am, that doesn't mean you sit and do nothing for three hours! But hopefully you get the idea. Be focused, disciplined and honest with yourself about what needs to be done ... then get on and do it.

One last thing: understand the difference between 'urgent' and 'important'. If you're not sure where a task fits, 'Eisenhower's Box' is a useful tool.

EISENHOWER'S BOX

American World War II General and later President, Dwight D. Eisenhower, was famous for being able to prioritise tasks. He accomplished this with a very simple system:

	URGENT	NOT URGENT
IMPORTANT	1 Pressing tasks with an imminent deadline	2 Personal development Making time for people
UNIMPORTANT	3 'Busywork' Most calls and email	4 Watching TV Checking social media

The idea is to spend as much time as possible working in box 2. If you're struggling to figure out what to do next, ask yourself which area of the box a particular job belongs. The crucial thing to note is that for most of us, the things that we would regard as the most important are also usually not very urgent, meaning they tend to get crowded out by urgent jobs. You might have 'spend quality time with my partner' on the list, which is obviously massively important. But it's not urgent. If you don't do it today, there's no immediate effect, so it's easy to put it off and convince yourself you can make up for it tomorrow. But tomorrow comes, and along with it comes another 'urgent' task, and the truly important tasks get postponed again ... and again ... and before you know it, a week goes by ... and then a month ...

Like many of the things we discuss in this book, there's no absolutes here – no black and white. It's all shades of grey. What can seem incredibly urgent one day may pale into insignificance the next – if someone you care about is unexpectedly taken ill, then repainting the spare room suddenly isn't such a big deal. It's also vital to remember that we all have different ideas about what is important. This is particularly relevant when other people assign us tasks. When someone else asks you to do something, it's crucial to consider not only how important that job is to you – but also how important the other *person* is to you. If your boss asks you to do something, your response should reflect your attitude to your boss, rather than the specific task she has set for you. Another example might be if your partner asks you to mow the lawn, as they don't have time. Well, maybe you hate cutting the grass and quite like that slightly wild look in your garden. But if your partner doesn't, then perhaps mowing the lawn goes further up your list than you might initially think. The importance and urgency of a job isn't just to do with how you feel, it's also about how it affects other people – especially when those people are important to you.

There is a balance to be struck here, and none of us get it right 100% of the time. But if we take the time to understand our values and decide to prioritise our time and tasks, then all of us can make better decisions.

WORKING EFFECTIVELY

"My powers are ordinary. Only my application brings me success."
Isaac Newton, 17th century English scientist

"Give me six hours to chop down a tree and I will spend the first four sharpening the axe." Abraham Lincoln, 19th century American statesman

Self-development is a skill like any other – if you want to get better, you have to practise. And consistent practice is rewarded with consistent improvement. How we work is a crucial element in this – quality is more important than quantity.

We've already talked about deciding on the most important jobs of the day. This is the first step, and means you don't slog your guts out for eight hours on stuff that has no real impact.

Once you have prioritised your tasks, try to set aside uninterrupted blocks of time to get those tasks completed. Research shows that after an interruption, it takes most people about 20 minutes to get back into the flow of working. It's not always possible, but if you can, then switch off the WiFi, put your phone on Airplane Mode, and focus completely on the task in hand for a set amount of time. Try to avoid 'working' at unspecified tasks for an unspecified time. This is a path to frustration! We've all been there – you get to the end of the day, and while you know you haven't sat around doing nothing ... you also can't quite put your finger on what you've accomplished that day.

If you work for yourself, the benefits of this are obvious – if you can GSD by lunchtime, you get to have the rest of the day off! But what if you work for someone else? Well, it's still important to work smart. Firstly, you'll get more job satisfaction – you'll feel better about yourself if you spend the day working on important tasks. Secondly, if you're being effective at work you are more likely to get noticed for promotions and pay rises. This can be hard to do – often your work environment doesn't feel like it's set up to reward people who put in more effort. Peer pressure comes in to play; if you're getting more done, your colleagues might start to make fun of the 'school swot'. Expect this. It's part of the deal. But know that you are destined for better things.

PERFECTIONISM
» PROCRASTINATION
» PARALYSIS

"A beautiful thing is never perfect." Egyptian proverb

There are three main causes of procrastination. When we are putting things off, we are usually telling ourselves one of the following:

1. That we don't quite know enough – we need to do some more research.

2. That the thing we've produced isn't quite good enough – it can be improved.

3. That we aren't quite good enough yet – we need to practice our skills a bit more.

When we are telling ourselves one of these stories, it can lead to what feels like a productive use of time. You read another book to learn some more ... or you spend another day making tiny tweaks to your product instead of actually

CHAPTER 5 :: Take Action

selling it to someone … or you do that training module one more time, just to be on the safe side.

But all the time we are telling ourselves we are 'making it better', we are putting off the really important thing – that one task that is actually going to make a real difference to us. Our search for perfection actually leads us into a world of procrastination, and if we're not careful, that can end up leaving us paralysed. Not only do we never quite get round to doing the most important thing, we end up doing nothing productive at all.

If that sounds familiar to you, remember that you are not alone. Almost everyone goes through this kind of battle with themselves at some point – for most people it's a daily occurrence! If you're trying to launch a new business, in the end you need to get your product or service in front of potential customers and see what they think. If you're trying to pluck up the courage to end a relationship, there will never be the perfect moment to do so. If you're trying to get healthy, then you need to start exercising today, not waiting until after the party you're going to at the weekend. If you're waiting for everything to be perfect, you'll be waiting forever.

One thing that can help is to develop an awareness of when you are actually doing useful work, as opposed to when you are doing 'busywork'. Busywork is when you're not lazing in front of the TV, you definitely spent the day 'working', but at the end of the day you can't quite put your finger on what you actually achieved. Learn to recognise the difference between busywork and GSD. When you are working, take a moment every now and then to ask yourself – "is this the most important thing for me to be doing right now?"

The answer to that question lies in understanding your values, and knowing what it is you are trying to achieve. Eisenhower's Box is brilliant for this. Busywork usually falls into the 'Urgent–but–not–important' box – or even worse, the 'Not–urgent–and–not–important' box. When you find yourself here, it's important not to beat yourself up. Do the opposite – congratulate yourself for noticing you're in the wrong box, decide what's really important, and get back on track.

Nobody ever truly 'defeats' procrastination – we all do it from time to time – but with practice you can reduce the amount of time you waste, and become much more productive.

> **'Why Procrastinators Procrastinate' [2013]**
> *Tim Urban*
> SUMMARY: A funny, practical guide to overcoming procrastination.
> KEY QUOTE: "Defeating procrastination is the same thing as gaining control over your own life."
>
> The way we can access personal development has been radically altered in the last couple of decades by the explosion of blogs and the arrival of TED talks. To do a talk for TED, someone needs to be a recognised expert, so you can be very confident of the quality and accuracy of information. Blogs are a bit different. Anyone can start one, so it pays to be selective – but the best ones are amazing resources. A fantastic example of this is the blog run by Tim Urban, called 'Wait But Why.' In it, Tim covers all kinds of topics from 'The Fermi Paradox' (pretty deep and intense), to 'How To Pick A Life Partner' (also pretty deep and intense), to '7 Ways to be Insufferable on Facebook' (rather less deep and intense!). He uses stick figures and lots of cartoons to illustrate his points, and he's also really funny. You barely realise how much you are actually learning!
>
> One of his most popular posts is called 'Why Procrastinators Procrastinate'. It has characters including the Instant Gratification Monkey and the Panic Monster, and is a piercingly accurate explanation of what procrastination is. It also has a ton of practical advice on how to combat it. If you find audio/visual learning more compelling, then his TED talk from 2016 called 'Inside the Mind of a Master Procrastinator' is equally brilliant.

With millions of views, it's in TED's Top 25 Most Watched, and is less than 15 minutes long. Watch it over breakfast. Or watch it twice instead of your favourite soap opera … I'll let you decide which of those two options has the bigger positive impact on your life …

Google 'Tim Urban Procrastination' to find them both.

(Just make sure you don't get there via "Oh, as I'm online, I'll quickly check Facebook first…")

"The problem with doing nothing is not knowing when you've finished." Benjamin Franklin, 18th century American polymath

MORE LIKE THIS: Two other excellent TED talks on related subjects are 'The Puzzle of Motivation' by Dan Pink and 'Your Elusive Creative Genius' by Elizabeth Gilbert. Find them all at www.ted.com

THE VALUE OF TIME

"Begin doing what you want to do now. We are not living in eternity. We have only this moment, sparkling like a star in our hand – and melting like a snowflake." Francis Bacon, 16th century English philosopher

"How we spend our days is, of course, how we spend our lives." Annie Dillard, 21st century American author

There are 168 hours in each week. Let's say you sleep 56 hours a week (8 hours a night), work 40 hours a week (Monday–Friday, 8 hours a day), and spend two hours a day on the essentials, like cooking, eating and showering. That still leaves 58 hours a week unaccounted for … You could have a second full–time job, and still have 2.5 hours a *day* to relax …

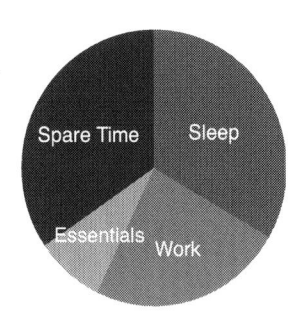

I know this is a simplistic example that misses out many things like your commute, or dropping the kids at school, but hopefully the point is clear. It's a useful (and often sobering) exercise to do for yourself. Make the effort to figure out exactly where your time goes each week, and see what you can learn from that. If you're having trouble working out where the time goes, you can try keeping a 'time diary' for a couple of weeks. Carry a small notebook everywhere, and note down what you do, and how long for. The more detailed the better … you'll probably be surprised at the results.

Very few people can account for every hour of their day, and even fewer can honestly say they make the most effective

CHAPTER 5 :: Take Action

use of that time. Look out for the time that seems to just 'disappear'. If you get in from work at 6, and have dinner at 7, do you really know what happens in that hour? It's OK if it is taken up with a bit of social media and mindless TV – as long as you're aware of it, and have decided to spend your time that way. Most of us have got more spare time than we think. This means that when we say "I don't have time for that", what we are actually saying is "that isn't a priority for me".

The 'Pareto Principle' (named after Italian economist Vilfredo Pareto), or '80/20 Law' is an important tool in time management. Pareto noted that in many areas of life about 80% of effects come from around 20% of causes. This means it is likely that 80% of your productivity is a result of 20% of your actions. Similarly, you may find that only about 20% of your actions are causing 80% of your challenges. It's not a hard and fast rule – sometimes the split might be 90/10, or 65/35, but it can be a useful tool to assess where you should invest more time, and where you might want to limit your efforts. Look at your 'time diary'. What are your most productive actions? And where are the points where it starts going a bit pear-shaped?

Another thing to do is see where you can use time more effectively. If you commute, can you read a good book on the train or listen to an educational podcast while you're stuck in traffic? What about while you're exercising? Or doing the washing up? When you start looking for them, you will find lots of nooks and crannies in your day where you can use your time more effectively.

No-one is suggesting that we should be crazy busy for the entire 16 or so hours that we are awake. It is important to make time to relax and recharge – but be honest with yourself about exactly how much time you spend doing that. If you are looking to make some changes in your life, it is crucial to figure out where you can make better use of your time. Understand that there's a good chance you'll need to make sacrifices in some areas.

TIME V MONEY

"Many people take no care of their money till they come nearly to the end of it, and others do just the same with their time." Johann Wolfgang von Goethe, 18th century German author

"The future is something which everyone reaches at the rate of sixty minutes an hour, whatever he does, whoever he is." C.S. Lewis, 20th century British writer

One of the biggest contrasts between rich and poor people is their attitude to the relationship between time and money. Poor people use time to save money. Rich people use money to save time. This sounds simple, but is an incredibly important point. It is possible to use both time and money more efficiently and effectively. The difference of course is that it is possible to generate more money, but no-one can create extra time. All of us have 24 hours in the day. Steve Jobs didn't have a magic machine that gave him an extra 8 hours a day that he used to build Apple. Leonardo Da Vinci and Benjamin Franklin had the same 24 hours as the rest of us. The concept of using money to leverage time is one that you can use without being a millionaire.

For many people, cleaning their house is one of the jobs they hate. As a simple example, let's say you can hire a cleaner for £10 an hour, and it takes three hours to clean your house – a total cost of £30. If you can fill those three hours with something that has more value than £30, then you should be paying someone else to clean your house. If you earn more than £10 an hour, then you could leverage the time to do more work. If you are paid £15 per hour, then working for two hours gives you the £30, and an extra hour you can use productively. There are other ways to measure 'value', of course. Perhaps you can spend those three hours with your partner – is that 'worth' more than £30 to you?

I understand that actual cash flow might be a problem for some people. Perhaps you only have a limited number of hours at work, and your wage barely covers the essentials. It may seem like the idea of using money to leverage your time is pie in the sky, or that it doesn't apply to you right now, but the concept is crucial to understand.

How can you leverage your time more effectively and efficiently to improve the quality of your life?

> **'The Power of Now' [1999]**
> *Eckhart Tolle*
> SUMMARY: A complex, spiritual book about living in the moment.
> KEY QUOTE: "Whatever the present moment contains, accept it as if you had chosen it."
>
> It's fair to say that Eckhart Tolle divides people. He has sold millions of books, and Oprah Winfrey is a fan, but 'Time' magazine described 'The Power of Now' as "mumbo jumbo". His writing style is an unusual combination. At times he is very direct. In answer to the question "How can we drop negativity?", Tolle's answer is: "By dropping it. How do you drop a piece of hot coal that you are holding in your hand?". In contrast to this, other passages require full attention, and it's not always easy to understand what he means. For example:
>
> *"The moment you realise you are not present, you are present. Whenever you are able to observe your mind, you are no longer trapped in it. Another factor has come in, something that is not of the mind: the witnessing presence."*
>
> Tolle's central message links Eastern and Western philosophies together, and for me the easiest way to understand his key concept is through a metaphor he uses in the book. Imagine you are stuck in the mud. At this exact moment – the 'Now' – there is little point worrying about how you got there, or what you might do if you ever get out. You need to accept your situation for what it is. This doesn't mean you don't take any action! You do of course make plans to escape from the mud, but Tolle

says that until we have calmly accepted the reality of our 'Now', anything else we do will be meaningless.

There are parallels both with Stoic ideas of acceptance, and Viktor Frankl's ideas about how we always get to choose our response in any given situation (see P28), but Tolle comes at it from a more spiritual angle.

It's a thought-provoking read, and if you enjoy his style then this book could well have an incredibly profound effect for you.

"Forever is composed of nows." Emily Dickinson, 19th century American poet

"The meeting of two eternities, the past and future ... is precisely the present moment." Henry David Thoreau, 19th century American author

MORE LIKE THIS: 'Chasing Daylight' by Eugene O'Kelly, 'Zen Mind, Beginner's Mind' by Shunryu Suzuki

'The GaryVee Audio Experience'
Gary Vaynerchuk

SUMMARY: Generally short, intense, business-led soundbites.

KEY QUOTE: "I'm driven by gratitude. Gratitude is my fuel."

The 'Audio Experience' team release a new podcast episode every day, with no particular theme running through — apart from Vaynerchuk's rapid-fire, no-nonsense delivery. Sometimes it's an interview, sometimes it's a Q&A or a keynote speech, and they can be any length from just a few minutes up.

Vaynerchuk is definitely one of the people that you have to be ready for. He's a brash New Yorker who curses all the time, and the first time I listened, I turned him off after less than five minutes. A couple of years went by, and I kept hearing his name so decided to give him another shot. I'm so, so glad I did as the episode from 25 May 2018 had a massive impact on me.

I've mentioned a few times how different people respond to things in different ways and at different times. I've shared that 25 May episode with so many people, and the usual response has been along the lines of "Yeah, I thought it was OK."

OK?! WTF?! That 15 minutes dragged me kicking and screaming out of a pretty deep slump I was in at the time (primarily procrastinating over getting this book finished), and I subsequently listened to it every day for over a month.

It might have the same effect on you ... but – truth be told – it almost certainly won't. And that's fine. You need to find what works for you.

When it comes to Gary Vee though, please bear this in mind. He's different to all the other resources I've mentioned, and you might need to listen to a few episodes to understand where he's coming from. His primary area of expertise is personal and corporate branding using social media, so for me to include him in a book on personal development might seem odd. However, his ethos is that any 'brand' has to be completely authentic, and so underneath his zero bullshit, machine gun delivery are a set of core principles that clearly determine his every move. His guiding values of gratitude, humility, and a ridiculous work ethic enable him to cut through any fluff, and focus on what really matters.

Give him a chance – he might just change your life.

"Gratitude is not only the greatest of the virtues, but the parent of all of the others." Marcus Tullius Cicero, Roman orator, 1st century BCE

> MORE LIKE THIS: 'Shut Up, Stop Whining and Get a Life' by Larry Winget, 'Why You're Dumb, Sick and Broke' by Randy Gage

HABITS

"We are what we repeatedly do. Excellence, then, is not an act but a habit." Will Durant, American author, 20th century (this quote is often misattributed to Aristotle)

Almost everything we do is a habit – some of them do us good, like cleaning our teeth, and some of them are maybe not so helpful – like having biscuits with every cup of tea you drink.

Our brain is an incredible thing. We each take around 20,000 breaths per day, and very rarely do we think about that. Our brain takes care of it for us, like it takes care of so many other things. Your subconscious brain is wired to take care of as many things as possible, leaving your conscious brain to work on the important stuff. The problem arises when we repeat something often enough that responsibility for it shifts from our conscious to our subconscious brain – we start doing something automatically, without really considering whether it's a good idea or not.

This can be with little, relatively unimportant things – perhaps you always play with your hair when you are thinking about something, but we can also easily fall into habits that aren't doing us much good. Like automatically switching on the TV when we get in from work.

The good news is that new habits are surprisingly easy to establish. There is a crucial mindset shift here: don't think about 'breaking bad habits' – that is concentrating too much on something negative (See P95 for more on this). Instead, when you want to change an aspect of your behaviour, focus on replacing it with something better. If you secretly know you eat too many biscuits every day (guilty as charged!), it probably won't work to still have the tea, but not have the biscuits. The 'tea and biscuits' are

CHAPTER 5 :: Take Action

too closely linked in your mind. Instead, go back a step, and replace the tea with a glass of water. Less interesting, admittedly, but much better for you. Bring it back to your values. If you value your health (and you definitely should), then cutting down the amount of caffeine and processed sugar (i.e. tea and biscuits) that you consume is much better for you. By looking at the bigger picture, you can weigh up the pros and cons more effectively, and give yourself a good reason why you should start a new habit.

The best thing about establishing good habits is that it doesn't take as long as you might think. Yes, it's tough for the first few days, and yes, you'll probably slip up occasionally – that's OK, just don't be too hard on yourself. Setting up a new habit takes approximately 20–30 days. Get disciplined for 3–4 weeks, and you can make a noticeable difference. Some people find that they can make lots of really big changes in one go, but others have more success starting with one small thing they want to change, then gradually adding other new habits as they make progress. You probably already know which of those two camps you fall into – but be honest with yourself. If you have a history of going crazy at the gym every January, but by Valentine's Day you're back on the sofa with a party pack of Doritos, then long-term you're probably going to have more success making smaller, more gradual changes.

One really good way to monitor your progress is to have some form of visual reference about how long your 'streak' has been going. Let's say you want to do ten push-ups every day. When you've done them, put a red tick on a calendar or wall chart. As the collection of ticks gets longer, the list itself becomes quite motivating! When you've done ten or twenty days in a row, not breaking your streak can be just as motivating as the health benefits from the push-ups. There are lots of good apps you can get for this, too. The one I use is called 'Done', and I have a list of about 15 daily tasks that I keep track of – everything from making my bed in the morning (see Admiral McRaven on P84), to having the WiFi off for two hours a day and reading 30 minutes a day.

It sounds a bit geeky, but it made a huge difference for me.

We are human beings, and habits are a huge part of our lives. Make certain that yours are working for you, and not against you.

"The diminutive chains of habit are scarcely ever heavy enough to be felt, till they are too strong to be broken." Maria Edgeworth, English author, 19th century

'Commencement Speech' [2014]
Admiral William H. McRaven

SUMMARY: Ten ideas for a more productive life.
KEY QUOTE: "If I have learned anything in my time travelling the world, it is the power of hope."

The next time you have 20 minutes spare, make yourself a cup of tea (no biscuits though!), grab your journal and a pen, and search for this speech on YouTube. You won't regret it.

McRaven is a US Navy SEAL, and his speech is about his time in training. It's got some incredible stories in it, and the way he weaves these into ten fundamental lessons on how to live a good life, and how that starts by doing the small things with care and consistency, is just fantastic. Lesson one is to start every day by making your bed, because "If you can't do the little things right, you'll never be able to do the big things right."

I never used to make my bed. Ever.

After watching this guy, I do it every single day. Without fail.

"Little by little does the trick." Aesop, Greek storyteller, 6th century BCE

MORE LIKE THIS: 'Stanford Commencement Speech [2005]' by Steve Jobs, 'Harvard Commencement Speech [2008]' by JK Rowling (find them all on YouTube)

SCREEN TIME

"It's not enough to be busy, so are the ants. The question is, what are we busy about?" Henry David Thoreau, 19th century American writer

On average, people in the UK spend around 27 hours a week watching television. That's more than a whole day. They also spend about 14 hours per week on their phones, and this number is rising fast.

Add those two numbers up, and it's pretty scary. 41 hours a week in front of a screen, on average. At the start of this chapter we looked at how you spend the 168 hours you get each week. If there was a big chunk unaccounted for, this is likely where they are.

Altering your screen habits could be the single biggest change you make. It might also be the most difficult! If you want to find out how addicted you are to your TV, go cold turkey. You'll quickly discover the depth of your addiction.

And if you want to get really serious, switch off the WiFi and put your phone on Airplane Mode at the same time …

OK – back to reality. I'm not really suggesting that you completely give up TV and your phone – but it is vital to have an honest understanding of exactly how much time you spend with these two things each week.

It's important to understand that the big companies want you to spend as much time with their products as possible, so they can sell advertising and make money. Research has shown that the 'Pull to Refresh' feature activates the same part of our brain that playing a fruit machine does. It's the same anticipation that something exciting might be about to happen, and it keeps us coming back for more. This is particularly important if you have kids. If your child was spending a couple of hours a day on a fruit machine, you'd probably have something to say about it. Society doesn't yet have the same view towards smartphone usage, but it's the same principle. Kids and adults are physically addicted to their phones. TV is the same – features like autoplaying the next episode are designed to keep us consuming content for as long as possible. This doesn't mean we can blame Facebook and Netflix for stealing our time! We still have to take personal responsibility for the amount of time we choose to spend in front of a screen.

This is not the place for a discussion about the social impact of TV and social media. For our purposes, the priority is to have a real understanding of how many hours you spend in front of a screen. Apps like 'Moment' and 'Rescue Time' can help you analyse and monitor the time you spend online and with your phone. You can then decide whether or not you are using those hours effectively.

Nowhere in any of the resources I've studied does a single person recommend spending more time in front of a screen. Yes, it's the 21st century, and I'm the first to admit that I love my laptop and phone, and the flexibility they give me. I've no intention of giving either of them up! But I try to use them as little as possible, and to use them as effectively as possible. If you bump into me at a train station, you may well find me mindlessly scrolling my life away … but I try really hard to keep that to a minimum.

It's not just about limiting the time we spend in front of screens. Another element of this is controlling what you consume. The overwhelming majority of the authors and speakers I've come across limit the amount of time they spend consuming the news, or the negativity, manipulation and shallowness of most TV and social media. Many cut it out completely. This is really hard to do, and it's OK to sometimes relax with a bit of mindless TV – but remember the old cliché: Garbage in, garbage out. If you eat junk food, your body suffers. It's the same with your mind. Your brain is the most sensitive and complex organ in your body, and you get to control what you feed it. Make sure you're giving it a healthy diet.

"I will not let anyone walk through my mind with their dirty feet." Mahatma Gandhi, 20th century Indian activist

ROUTINE

Eventually your habits become routines. They are an integral part of living your life the best way you can. The ones that are important and meaningful will be different for everybody, so here I'm just going to introduce a few ideas. Pick and choose the ones that feel right to you. If one of them makes you uncomfortable – if it seems like it would be too far out of your comfort zone – remember to ask yourself why that is. Remind yourself that the only way we grow is to step out of our comfort zones.

DAILY

"Every morning we are born again. What we do today is what matters most." Gautama Buddha, Indian sage, 5th century BCE

"And never say of anything, 'Indeed, I will do that tomorrow.'" The Qur'an

Many people find that starting every day off in the exact same way is a good idea. Tony Robbins calls it 'Priming'. You are spending a few minutes getting each of your body, mind and spirit ready for the day ahead. As you start to read and listen to different people, you will get ideas for things that might work for you, but common morning practices include:

- BEING GRATEFUL. Think about (or write down) three things that you are grateful for. This is easy for the first few days, but can easily get repetitive (the summer sun, my amazing family, fresh coffee, and so on), so try to think broadly. Think about people, objects and places. Think about the past, present and future. Think about lessons you've learned and experiences you've had. Spend a few seconds really being grateful for each of the three things.

- AFFIRMATIONS. It's easy to be sceptical about the effectiveness of affirmations, but they come up often enough to be worth mentioning. This is really about putting yourself in a positive frame of mind to start the day. Affirmations start with "I am …", but then become very personal to you. They may be based on your values and/or mission statement, and it might take a while to discover the ones that feel right to you. Once you find them, they tend to stay pretty constant. Remember to keep the language positive – say: "I am healthy". Don't be negative – don't say: "I am not fat".

- REVIEW YOUR GOALS. If you have your goals written down somewhere, spend a few moments reading over them to remind yourself why you do what you do, and what the next steps are.

- JOURNAL. Jot down a couple of sentences each morning about how you are feeling. Sometimes this will feel a bit pointless, but on other days it can really help get things straight in your head. If you wake up feeling particularly unmotivated, you can try a 'Stream of Consciousness'. (See P134 for more details).

- MAKE YOUR BED. This isn't really about having a

neatly made bed. It's more about the mindset of starting each day with a task completed, which then carries over into the rest of the day. If you don't already make your bed each morning, try it for a month and see if you notice the difference.

- EXERCISE. This doesn't have to mean going for a run every morning (although that IS a really good way to start the day). Even if you just do a few stretches, push-ups and crunches for a couple of minutes, do something to wake your muscles up in the morning.

- MEDITATE. The number of successful people who meditate every day is extraordinary. Even more amazing is how many of them can link starting a meditation practice with becoming more effective. See P132 for a couple of simple meditations you can try.

- COLD SHOWER. Don't knock it until you've tried it! A 15–30 second blast of cold water at the end of your shower will definitely wake you up! There is some evidence that suggests it also increases your white blood cell count, enabling you to better resist illness. If you're interested in the benefits of cold water, Google Wim Hof (a Dutch guy who hiked to the death zone on Everest in shorts and sandals. Seriously) and/or Laird Hamilton (an American big wave surfer who runs intense health retreats at his home in Hawaii).

Start with a couple that make sense to you, and go from there. Setting yourself up for the day will definitely reap rewards.

It is also beneficial to end your day with some positive action, rather than just falling asleep on the sofa. Here are a few ideas:

- SCREENS OFF. More evidence is amassing showing that the type of light emitted by our phones, tablets and TVs actually keeps us awake, rather than helping us sleep. Try making the hour before you go to sleep screen free, and see if you notice any difference in the quality of your sleep. (And not just after a day or two. You need to try this for a couple of weeks to see the benefits).

- READ TEN PAGES. End your day with something positive and beneficial, rather than the misery and violence of TV news channels.

- WHAT MADE TODAY GREAT? Much like noting the things you are grateful for in the morning, at the end of the day spend a few moments reflecting on three things that happened today that made it a brilliant day. This could be anything from finishing a big project, to some food you enjoyed, to the friendly smile that shop assistant gave you.

- TOMORROW'S TOP THREE. Write down the three most important things you want to get done tomorrow. By doing this the evening before, you don't have to procrastinate over it in the morning. You can get stuck straight in to the first task.

- PLAN TOMORROW. Now you know your top three tasks, spend a moment planning the day, and working out when the jobs will get done. And if you can get them done by midday ... then it's OK to give yourself the rest of the day off.

- MEDITATE. Taking 10–20 minutes every evening to calm your brain down before bed can really improve your sleep. Again, if you're sceptical about meditation, have a look at Tim Ferriss' 'Tools of Titans', and notice how many of those 100+ top performers – from all walks of life – make the time to meditate twice a day.

- ASK YOUR BRAIN A QUESTION. Before you go to sleep, ask your brain to help you solve a problem. This might sound a bit crazy, but our subconscious minds are continually beavering away in the background. You've probably experienced it – that moment when the solution to something you've been struggling with suddenly comes to you. While you're resting your physical body with sleep, get your brain to carry on working. It might just surprise you ... Keep a notebook and pen by the side of your bed. When you wake up in the middle of the night with a brilliant idea, write it down. Guaranteed you won't remember it in the morning. Of course, in the cold light of day, it might not seem like such a brilliant idea after all, but you never know ...

WEEKLY

One simple way to increase your productivity is to plan your week in advance. This sounds a bit geeky, but actually only takes a few minutes to do, and will make you much more efficient. Most people will do this on a Sunday evening, but it makes no difference – as long as you put aside a regular time to do it.

You'll need a planner of some sort – the Action Diary is great for this, as it has different areas for tasks and projects, as well as a weekly planner divided into hourly time slots. Alternatively, you can use a regular diary, or a worksheet of some sort – the important thing is that you can see the whole week in one go. Whichever method you use, all you now do is take 10 minutes on a Sunday to fill in the stuff that you already know about. This could be appointments, the school play, or jobs that need doing. It's important to timetable the jobs – don't just add 'mow the lawn' to your to-do list. Mark in your planner exactly *when* you are going to mow the lawn. Once you've got it all down on paper you can see where the gaps are – the times when you can relax, or add in the 'important–but–not–urgent' tasks (see Eisenhower's Box on P70).

This is one of those things that is easy to do – and also

really easy not to do. But planning your week this way ensures you always find time for the things that are truly important to you.

MONTHLY

A really good routine to get into is find an hour or so at the end of each month to review your goals in detail. Hopefully you're having a quick scan of them a couple of times a day, but it's an excellent idea to get into the habit of studying them in a bit more detail on a monthly basis.

Are you on schedule to learn that skill or complete that goal? If not, why not? Can you catch up, or do you need to adjust the deadline slightly? Be honest with yourself here – but don't be too brutal! There's a fine line between acknowledging when you've perhaps been a bit slack, and appreciating that actually, it just turned into a really busy month and so you've had to delay things a bit.

If you find that there's a particular goal that you don't seem to be progressing on, ask yourself why. It's likely that the goal sounds good on paper, but actually doesn't motivate you for some reason. If that's the case, it's fine to put it to one side – or maybe get rid of it completely. As you live your life, it's completely natural that your priorities will change. As they do, adjust your objectives to reflect that.

YEARLY

You know that weird week between Christmas and New Year that usually disappears in a haze of cold turkey and picking up bits of tinsel from the floor? That is the perfect opportunity to do a yearly review! Skim back through your journal and/or diary, and notice what went well – and what maybe didn't go so well. Spend an evening making a few notes, and see what you can learn from it. Make a simple list – on one side write down the good things, on the other, put the things that drained you. See if there are any recurring themes – if lots of your happy memories surround a particular person or group of people, then make sure you spend more time with them next year. And vice-versa. If you find that your challenges mostly revolved around a particular situation, then try to reduce the time you spend in that environment. (You will probably find the '80/20 Law' comes into effect here. See P77).

With these lists in hand, you can start to map out the upcoming year. There will of course be many things – holidays, birthdays, anniversaries, etc – that you can mark up a long way in advance. But also spend some time reflecting on your values and long-term goals.

Ask yourself – what do I need to do so that this time next year I'm reflecting on what an awesome year I've had?

CHAPTER 6 :: COMMUNICATION

TALKING TO YOURSELF

"The more man meditates upon good thoughts, the better will be his world and the world at large." Confucius, Chinese philosopher, 6th century BCE

"If you hear a voice within you say 'you cannot paint,' then by all means paint, and that voice will be silenced." Vincent Van Gogh, 19th century Dutch painter

"Talk to yourself like you would to someone you love." Brené Brown, 21st century American writer

COMMUNICATION STARTS WITH HOW WE talk to ourselves. What is the internal dialogue like, and how does it affect us in our everyday lives?

The idea of 'talking to yourself' is usually seen a sign of being a bit loopy. But actually we all have an almost continuous internal dialogue going on. "Oh crap, why did I say that to her? I bet she thinks I'm a complete numpty now" … "What did he really mean when he told me about his new job? Maybe I should get a new job?" … "I'm so lazy, I really need to eat better and exercise more" … "Am I a good parent? Do my kids even like me?" … and so on.

The truth is that we spend most of our time listening to our internal voice, and that it talks down to us in a way that we would never dream of talking to anyone else. We are incredibly harsh, constantly berating ourselves for not being attractive enough, or smart enough, or healthy enough, or funny enough, or whatever it is. Learning to recognise the way we talk to ourselves, and understanding the damage it can do is a vital part of the self-development journey. There have been numerous reports and studies on the power of positive self-talk – most notably in sports. Every top athlete these days understands the importance of believing in themselves first and foremost, which then leads on to using visualisation to 'see' in your imagination the outcomes you want from any given situation.

Before you think about competing in the next Olympics, however, we first have to get the chatter in our heads under control!

The first step is simply to recognise it is happening. The next time you find your head saying "You're not good enough", just acknowledge that it is happening. Don't try and shut it out – that won't work; none of us can just turn this stuff off. Simply notice that you are being mean to yourself. It sounds a bit weird, but it really does work.

The next stage is to shift the negative self–talk to something positive. Understand that your brain is trying to help – that's why those voices originally evolved. They are our most primal instincts, trying to keep us out of harm's way. For most of our history, human beings have lived in a really dangerous world and it was our brain's job to protect us. The world we live in has moved on from that, but some parts of our brains have not evolved fast enough to keep up with the changes. Sometimes, this can be really useful to us … but other times, well, the messages from our brain are a bit outdated and can end up holding us back. When the negative self–talk begins, respond by telling yourself that you *are* good enough, that you *do* have the skills needed for this task, and after a time you will find that your instinctive brain starts to calm down.

Depending on how loud and aggressive your particular internal voice is, you might find that you sometimes have to be quite firm with it! There have been times when I have been screaming abuse at myself. "NO! You're ******* wrong! I AM good enough for this, so shut the **** up, and **** off! I don't ******* need you right now!" (So far as I'm aware, up until now I've always managed to keep this in my head …) You may not have to be as extreme as this, but you do need to respond when the negative self–talk begins.

Mantras can be really useful here – short, positive

CHAPTER 6 :: Communication

affirmations that you repeat over and over in your head. The wording is important. For example, if your negative self-talk is "I am fat", you don't want to change it to "I am NOT fat" – your subconscious will still focus on the word 'fat'. Instead, gently say to yourself "I am healthy". Notice how this is different to goals, where we want to be specific. When we are trying to get specific tasks done, it's another part of the brain – one that needs details in order to function. The negative self-talk originates in a different, more primal, part of the brain. Calming it down needs broader, more general statements.

I know what you're thinking. What a load of nonsense ... The reality is, however, that the power of changing your self-talk has been demonstrated time and again, in study after study.

There's a really important caveat here though – one that we've already come back to time and time again. Just changing your self-talk alone isn't enough. You can say "I am healthy" as many times as you want, but if you keep eating those chocolate bars, well, not much is going to change! You need to combine your positive self-talk with positive action. And the reason this is important is that if you don't change the self-talk – if your head keeps telling you you're fat – then it won't be long before you give up on that new eating and training routine.

If you want to make changes, you have to change both your mind and your actions.

"Watch your thoughts; they become words. Watch your words; they become actions. Watch your actions; they become habit. Watch your habits; they become character. Watch your character; it becomes your destiny." Lao Tzu, Chinese philosopher, 5th century BCE

"Your life is what your thoughts make it." Marcus Aurelius, 2nd century Roman philosopher

"Whatever the mind can conceive and believe, it can achieve." Napoleon Hill, 20th century American writer

'How to Win Friends and Influence People' [1937]
Dale Carnegie

SUMMARY: One of the classics; still relevant, and a fairly easy read.

KEY QUOTE: "People don't criticise themselves for anything, no matter how wrong it may be."

This is one of the legendary books from this era, along with Napoleon Hill's 'Think and Grow Rich' (see P22). Carnegie's book is significantly more accessible than Hill's, and don't let the title put you off. It sounds like it's going to be a morally suspect book about manipulating people to get your own way … and sometimes it is a bit like that. However, Carnegie also repeatedly reminds the reader that being genuine is the number one priority, and that none of the ideas will work if people don't like and trust you. He advocates taking action, and is constantly reminding the reader where they need to do the most work:

"Do you know someone you would like to change and regulate and improve? Good! That is fine. I am all in favour of it. But why not begin on yourself? From a purely selfish standpoint, that is a lot more profitable than trying to improve others – yes, and a lot less dangerous."

Stylistically, it is more accessible than 'Think and Grow Rich', but you will still find some of the language and phrasing to be quite old fashioned. It also has some of the underlying sexism and racism that many of the books from this era contain. This is a reflection of the times as much as Carnegie's views. It's important to remember that we are all a product of our upbringing and surroundings to some extent, and an analysis of whether the ideas we grow up with are serving us in the best way is ultimately what our personal development journey is all about. 'How to Win Friends' is a good example of how some of the details have changed, but the underlying principles remain the same.

Carnegie's book has sold many millions of copies, and is still in print many decades after its initial publication. For this reason, it really is one of the 'must read' self-development resources out there. You may not agree with all he says, but whatever you end up thinking of it, the book is an important part of the self-development world. It's worth being familiar with it.

"Everyone thinks of changing the world, but no one thinks of changing himself." Leo Tolstoy, Russian author, 19th century

MORE LIKE THIS: 'Tribes' by Seth Godin, 'Legacy' by James Kerr

LISTENING

"The fool speaks, the wise man listens." Ethiopian proverb

"You only know me as you see me, not as I actually am." Immanuel Kant, 17th century German philosopher

Some years ago, a very close friend of mine was diagnosed with cancer. I was there when they found out, and as we were leaving the hospital a Macmillan nurse pressed a short leaflet into my hand. It was called 'Lost for Words: How to talk to someone with cancer'. It contained one incredibly powerful line which has been emblazoned in my mind ever since.

"Listening is not the same as waiting to speak."

Please read that line again.
And once more for luck.

That line contains the basis of all effective communication. People want to be heard. It is crucially important to take the time to really listen to people, and fully understand what they are trying to say before we attempt to put our own point of view across. Of all the things I talk about in this book, this is probably the one that I struggle with the most.

I look back, and there are so many times when I have been so keen to tell the world what I think, that I have had no patience with what the person in front of me is trying to say. I still have a long way to go, but since I read that line I've definitely got better – and the difference it has made in all my interactions has been wonderfully profound.

In his '7 Habits', Stephen R. Covey's fourth habit is 'Seek First to Understand, Then to Be Understood'. When people are talking, it is surprisingly rare that they are really listened to. If you become the person who truly listens with empathy, you will shoot up in their estimation, and they will be much more likely to listen to you in return.

It's important that you don't confuse the 'empathic listening' that we are talking about here with 'active listening'. 'Active listening' is mentioned in a lot of books, and they suggest nodding your head, making eye contact and encouraging "mmm" or "ohh" sounds to make the speaker believe you are really paying attention to everything they are saying. Those physical indications from the listener are a part of 'empathic listening' – but the difference is intention. With 'active listening', you want the speaker to *think* they are being paid attention to in order that you can ultimately say your piece and have your way. With 'empathic listening', you are *truly* paying attention. You are absorbing and understanding what is being said, and – crucially – you are open to changing your views and opinions as a result of what is being said. 'Active listening' is a technique. 'Empathic listening' is a genuine desire to understand.

In a situation where there is likely to be disagreement, it is incredibly powerful for the listener to give a short summary of what has been said before voicing their own opinion. This does three things. Firstly, it proves that attention was being paid. Secondly, it demonstrates that you have understood correctly. And thirdly, it reduces the chances of disagreements escalating into arguments. Often, arguments happen because there is a lack of understanding – the conflict is about not being listened to rather than about the principles or ideas being discussed. If both sides can demonstrate that they listened and understood, it is possible to disagree without the situation deteriorating into antagonism.

If you need to start a difficult conversation with someone, it can be a good idea to frame it in terms of how it made you feel, rather than what the other person did. It's really hard to do this without getting some sort of accusation in there – some reference to 'you' – but adding an 'I' as well can make it seem like it's a problem to be solved together rather than an individual character flaw that is being highlighted. For example, if you have a friend who is frequently late, you might say:

"When I have to wait for someone at a cafe, it makes me feel really uncomfortable – I know it's a bit daft, but I always think that I've got the wrong day or something. I get really nervous."

There is still a testing conversation to be had, but it can be a better place to start than "You're so disorganised. Why are you always late?"

It's important not to use ideas like these as manipulative tools. The aim here isn't to always have your way, or get one over on someone, it's to improve the relationship for everyone. People will soon see through it if you start trying to manipulate them.

"When you talk, you are only repeating what you already know. But when you listen, you may learn something new." JP McEvoy, 20th century American writer (this quote is often misattributed to the Dalai Lama)

> **'Men Are From Mars, Women Are From Venus' [1992]**
> *John Gray*
> SUMMARY: An easy to read relationship guide
> KEY QUOTE: "A relationship requires that partners communicate their changing feelings and needs. To expect perfect communication is certainly too idealistic. Fortunately, between here and perfection

there is a lot of room for growth."

This is a book that has sold millions and gets consistently high reviews on Amazon, but one that is also easy to criticise. The central message is that men and women think and see the world differently – and it's very easy to say "well, duh! Of course they do! We all know that!" The problem is that while we all know that, we don't all behave like that. Many of us judge a situation from our own point of view, and aren't that great at understanding how it might be perceived differently by someone else. This is particularly true of the male/female dynamic, where the starting points are quite different. Essentially, Gray says that men primarily need to feel appreciated, accepted and trusted, while women value feeling cared for, understood and respected.

Before you switch off or write letters of complaint, it's important to know that Gray acknowledges the broadness of this generalisation. It might apply to the majority, but that certainly doesn't mean everybody is the same – we're a lot more complicated than that!

For relationships that do fall into his definitions, there are lots of practical suggestions for how you can manage your language and behaviour in order to better support the other person, and hopefully avoid misunderstandings. Stylistically, his division of the male and female roles into the Mars and Venus framework might be a bit simplistic and dated for some readers. Nonetheless, if this is an area where you sometimes struggle, approach it with an open mind and you may well find this a very useful book.

"It is not our differences that divide us. It is our inability to recognise, accept, and celebrate those differences." Audre Lorde, 20th century American activist

MORE LIKE THIS: 'Emotional Intelligence' by Daniel Goleman, 'Radical Acceptance' by Tara Brach

CHAPTER 6 :: Communication

SEVEN WORDS

THANK YOU

"Reflect upon your present blessings, of which every man has plenty; not on your past misfortunes, of which all men have some." Charles Dickens, 19th century English writer

Too often we take people for granted. We stop noticing all the things they are doing for us. We might remember to say thanks for the big things – the birthday presents, the anniversary dinner – but we very quickly accept the little things that people do for us as being a normal part of our everyday lives. When we take people for granted, they can quickly – and rightly – become resentful. If we are not careful, that resentment can build and build and eventually lead to much more serious issues. Remember to say thank you, and make an effort when you do – take their hand or give them a hug as you remind them how brilliant they are.

Saying "thank you" often goes hand in hand with "I'm sorry":

"I'm sorry I'm late. Thanks for your patience."

"Sorry I forgot to take the bins out. Thank you for reminding me."

When we apologise, it's about us – we say "I" – but when we express gratitude to the other person, we are acknowledging the positive contribution they have made to the situation, as well as our own failings.

Express your gratitude authentically, and whenever you can.

I'M SORRY

"Never ruin an apology with an excuse." Benjamin Franklin, 18th century American polymath

We all make mistakes. Most of the time, we make many more mistakes than we like to admit. Taking ownership of our mistakes – taking personal responsibility for them – is a vitally important thing to do. Once we have either realised our mistake or had it brought to our attention, there are two things we need to do. Firstly, we must apologise. Secondly, we must make the effort to correct the actions that led to the mistake in the first place. The apology is ultimately meaningless without taking steps to change our behaviour.

No-one is saying it's easy. It's not. Admitting we messed up is a really hard thing to do. We also need to make sure we apologise with sincerity. There's nothing worse than saying "I'm sorry for not taking the bins out, BUT I was tired." Don't add an excuse or justification – it completely negates the sincerity of the apology.

"I'm sorry I did that. Thank you for bringing it to my attention. I'm going to do my best to make sure I don't do that again, but if I do, please let me know."

Take ownership of your mistakes, and have the courage to apologise for them.

I LOVE YOU

"Being deeply loved by someone gives you strength, while loving someone deeply gives you courage." Lao Tzu, Chinese philosopher, 5th century BCE

"Darkness cannot drive out darkness: only light can do that. Hate cannot drive out hate: only love can do that." Martin Luther King Jr, 20th century American activist

If I need to explain why this is important, then the help you need is probably beyond the realms of this book. I don't mean to sound flippant – I really mean that. Yes, we can demonstrate our love with our actions, and that is a really important thing to do, but in the end we all need to hear the words as well. Like many things, this is equally true the other way around: we can say "I love you" twenty times a day, but if our actions aren't demonstrating that love, then the words quickly become meaningless.

As human beings we all need to feel connected to other people, and these three words demonstrate that connection like no others. It can be incredibly hard to tell someone you love them – it makes us vulnerable to being hurt. But if it's true, then it is always the right thing to do.

When you love someone, tell them.

These seven words can improve all of our relationships, but always remember that actions speak louder than words. We can't use these words to try and manipulate people to get our own way, or to get away with things. We can say "thanks" and "I'm sorry" and "I love you" a thousand times, and a thousand times more, but they will ultimately seem hollow and empty if our behaviour doesn't reflect our words. If we are habitually late, in the end it won't matter how often we apologise – the other person will eventually see through us. The apology becomes worthless – and then when we really need to apologise for a major mistake we make, we won't be believed. We've broken the trust with our repeated minor transgressions.

Thank you. I'm sorry. I love you.

Gratitude. Humility. Love.

These seven words represent three concepts with the power to change all of your relationships. Use them wisely, and use them often.

CHAPTER 7 :: LEADERSHIP

WHAT IS LEADERSHIP

"We are the leaders we have been waiting for." Native American saying

DEFINING 'LEADERSHIP' IS A BIT like trying to define what makes a 'good person'. Instinctively, we all know how to be a good person, but framing and describing it is a bit more tricky. Leadership is the same. Take a look at the following list – who here do you think of as being a leader?

Nelson Mandela	Mother Teresa
Jessica Ennis–Hill	Cristiano Ronaldo
J.K. Rowling	Mahatma Gandhi
Martin Luther King Jr	Emma Watson
Richard Branson	Anita Roddick
Mark Zuckerberg	Steve Jobs
Margaret Thatcher	Winston Churchill
Michelle Obama	Bob Geldof
Arnold Schwarzenegger	Princess Diana

The answers clearly won't be the same for everyone, but think of the people you admire. What connects them? What do they have in common? What does leadership mean to you?

We can definitely say it's not the same as being a 'boss'. It's not ordering other people around and getting them to do what you want them to. People follow a leader because they want to, not because they have to. They see something in that person that inspires them, that makes them believe they can be a better person, that they are important – that they can have an impact.

You may not have given it much thought, but your school days almost certainly gave you examples of good leadership. How did you feel about the teachers that shouted and screamed at the class? The ones that expected you to do something just because the teacher said so. I doubt you look back on them with any respect, fondness or admiration. On the other hand, if you were lucky enough to have a brilliant teacher at some point, reflect on how they made you feel. Chances are you worked harder in that lesson because you wanted to, not because you had to. Because that teacher inspired you. And when that brilliant teacher had to tell an individual or class off, they probably weren't angry – more likely they were disappointed. Probably you felt the same way – you didn't resent that teacher … you understood – you may even have felt guilty because you let them down.

Leadership in life works the same way. Whether it's at work, in a sports team, or in your family, great leaders are there to inspire and lift up the people around them.

LEAD YOURSELF

"Example is not the main thing in influencing others. It is the only thing." Albert Schweitzer, 20th century French–German writer

Before you can lead anyone else, you have to be able to lead yourself. You need to be able to look objectively at your actions and decisions, and know whether or not you've done your best. And if you haven't … then you must be honest with yourself, and hold yourself to a higher standard.

There is a balance to be struck here. On one level, nothing is ever perfect – there's always something we can do to improve. There's no value in constantly beating yourself up over every last little detail – that will ultimately be counter–productive. Generally, deep down you'll know whether you've put enough effort into a project, relationship, or whatever ... and if your gut is saying you could have done better, then you need to listen to that. Make the necessary adjustments, and resolve to improve.

As you get better at this the people around you will start to notice, and you will begin to lead by example. As you begin to hold yourself accountable to higher standards, this will rub off on the people you spend time with, and they will be lifted up to a higher level.

Sometimes, leading by example is all you need to do in order to start a movement. Google Derek Sivers 'Lone Nut' for a short, fun video that demonstrates this. It starts with one person dancing like a crazy person in a field at a festival and ... well, you'll have to watch the video to see what happens next!

The important thing to understand is that all movements start with one person – and that could be you.

"Be the change you want to see in the world." Mahatma Gandhi, 20th century Indian activist

LEAD OTHERS

"If not me, who? If not now, when?" Hillel the Elder, Jewish sage, 1st century BCE

Leading other people starts with you stepping up. Usually, you have recognised a problem that needs to be solved, and you then decide to stick your head above the parapet and say "I've got this". Occasionally you might get involved with a project, and one day suddenly realise that you're the one with their head sticking out!

However it happens, the most obvious thing to say is that if you're the one who sticks their neck out, you're also the one who is going to be the target when things start to get challenging. This means you need to have a certain degree of self–confidence – but it absolutely doesn't mean you need to know everything. If you try to control every last detail, you become a dictator ... You won't find any of the personal development figures suggesting that as a good option! Trying to do it all will also result in you being overwhelmed, and making bad decisions. Good leaders understand the strengths and weaknesses of themselves, and the team around them, and utilise them all.

"If you want to go quickly, go alone. If you want to go far, go together." African proverb

'Start With Why' [2009]
Simon Sinek
SUMMARY: An analysis of how great leaders inspire the people around them.
KEY QUOTE: "Finding why is a process of discovery, not invention."

This book has become a global phenomenon. Sinek's TED talk outlining the central concepts in the book is one of their most watched videos ever.

Sinek's idea centres on what he calls 'The Golden Circle':

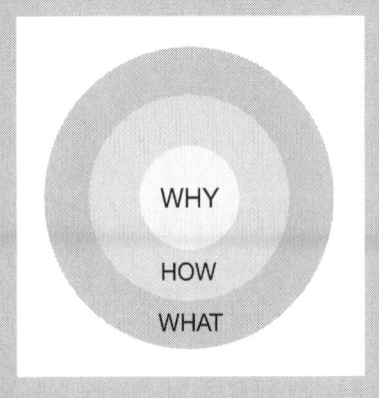

```
WHY
HOW
WHAT
```

In the centre is our 'why' – the fundamental reasons why we do what we do. The middle band is 'how' we do things, and the outer ring is 'what' we actually do. Sinek's observation is that most of us work from the outside–in – what, how, then why. We get so wrapped up in what we are doing, and how we go about it, that we never get round to figuring out *why* – which is the most important part. What we should be doing is starting in the centre – understanding our 'why' is the first thing we need to do. This then helps us decide how to act, and finally work out what we need to do. Sinek develops the concept, and talks extensively about how effective leaders need to have a concrete understanding of their 'why' in order to inspire the people around them.

My suggestion would be to watch the TED talk first. It's very good, and clearly explains his ideas. Then, if you decide you want to dig a bit deeper, get a copy of the book.

"First I will think. Then I will act." Inscription on the tomb of Darius of Persia, 5th century BCE

MORE LIKE THIS: 'Outliers' by Malcolm Gladwell, 'What Should I Do With My Life' by Po Bronson

STRENGTHS AND WEAKNESSES

"If all things were equally in all men, nothing would be prized." Thomas Hobbes, 17th century English philosopher

"My strength and my weakness are twins in the same womb." Marge Piercy, 20th century American poet

Very often, our greatest strengths are also our greatest weaknesses, and vice versa. Perhaps one of your strengths is making quick decisions. There are undoubtedly times when that is an incredibly useful skill to have. But there are also times when your ability to make snap decisions might lead to you dismissing other people's ideas without giving them enough thought and attention. You might miss something crucial – and you will almost certainly make the other person feel undervalued and unappreciated.

On the other side of the coin, perhaps you see yourself as quiet and introverted, and regard that as a weakness.

Turn that idea on it's head. It probably also means that you notice details in things that other people miss. You will have different knowledge and a different perspective on things, which can be incredibly valuable.

Whether you regard yourself as a leader or have aspirations to do so, it can be incredibly powerful to reframe strengths and weaknesses in this way. Understand how the perceived 'strengths' of both yourself and the people around you could lead to potential problems ... Understand also how perceived 'weaknesses' can often bring unforeseen benefits. Take some time to think about how your personal strengths might sometimes be causing you problems, and also how you might turn your 'weaknesses' to your advantage.

"The world breaks everyone, and afterward, some are strong at the broken places." Ernest Hemingway, 20th century American novelist

ROLE MODELS

"Imagine for yourself a character, a model personality, whose example you determine to follow, in private as well as in public." Epictetus, 1st century Greek philosopher

Like dreams, many of us give up on having heroes as we grow up. As an adult, the idea of looking up to someone seems childish. I'm not suggesting anyone starts worshipping their favourite movie star, putting posters on the wall and that sort of thing, but looking at the people we admire and seeing what we can learn from them can be an incredibly valuable process.

There are a number of different ways we can learn about successful people. Biographies and autobiographies are an obvious place to start. Generally, they reveal that any success a person may have had comes from hard work and dedication, and that everyone gets it wrong sometimes. Some successful people get it wrong a lot!

We each have our own heroes – we all have different things we struggle with and want to learn about. Write a list of the people you admire, and use this as a starting point.

See what you can discover about them, and what lessons you can learn. Pay particular attention to any 'overnight success stories' that might be on your list. Research them, and you will almost always discover that they put in years of work before achieving significant success.

You will probably want to follow your own thoughts here, but a few people's journeys that I have enjoyed discovering include:

JESSICA ENNIS
'Unbelievable' was written after her success at the London Olympics, and is a fantastic and easily-read story of how a small girl from Sheffield became an Olympic icon.

ELIZABETH GILBERT
'Eat Pray Love' was a global phenomenon. In it, Gilbert bares the darkest corners of her soul as she travels the world to figure out life after her divorce.

STEVE JOBS
Any of Walter Isaacson's books are worth reading, but his biography of Steve Jobs is a surprisingly open and honest account of a complex genius.

NELSON MANDELA
'Long Walk to Freedom' is not for the faint-hearted! It's very long, detailed, and intense. It's ultimately worth the effort – but I highly recommend reading 'Nelson Mandela: Portrait of an Extraordinary Man' first.

'Nelson Mandela: Portrait of an Extraordinary Man' [2010]
Richard Stengel

SUMMARY: Inspirational read about Nelson Mandela's personal philosophies.

KEY QUOTE: "I learned that courage was not the absence of fear, but the triumph over it. The brave man is not he who does not feel afraid, but he who conquers that fear."

Stengel worked closely with Nelson Mandela on 'Long Walk To Freedom', Mandela's autobiography. That book is the incredible story of an extraordinary man – but it does have one slight issue. Mandela is so humble and unassuming that it's easy to come away from the book underestimating the man himself.

Stengel fills that gap brilliantly with 'Portrait of an Extraordinary Man'. The chapter titles read like a 'how to' of personal development – 'Be Measured', 'Have a Core Principle', 'It's a Long Game' and 'Find Your Own Garden' are a few examples. As one of the greatest leaders the world has ever seen, there is a huge amount of inspiration and practical knowledge to be gained from reading this fantastic book.

What comes across primarily is that Mandela was a man of principle. He believed in equality for all, and sacrificed his liberty and – to a certain extent – his relationships with his family in pursuit of that principle. What also comes through is that he was a man a great discipline – exercising regularly (especially while in prison), and constantly working to improve his knowledge and understanding. He was also a pragmatist. His core principles never wavered, but it is very interesting to see how his tactics and strategies varied greatly over time, and were dependent on the specific circumstances at the moment.

CHAPTER 7 :: Leadership

> As Shane Parrish at the Farnam Street blog puts it, self-development is about "mastering the best of what other people have already figured out". Mandela was one of the greatest leaders the world has ever seen, and the opportunity to access some of his wisdom is one none of us should miss.
>
> *"How wonderful it is that nobody need wait a single moment before starting to improve the world." Anne Frank, 20th century German diarist*

FEAR AND FAILURE

"Our greatest glory lies not in never falling, but in rising every time we fall." Confucius, Chinese philosopher, 6th century BCE

Most of us are scared to fail. At first glance, this seems like a sensible attitude to have – and in many ways it is. If something seems big and scary, why would any sane person choose to put themselves in a position to mess it up, to potentially be embarrassed in front of other people? Fear is a natural human response to a challenging situation, and anyone who tells you they don't feel fear is either lying, stupid, or both!

Shifting your mindset on failure is one of the most important changes you can make. Too many people think that at a certain point in our lives, we reach a fork in the road. One path leads to success, the other to disaster. We end up paralysed with doubts and fears, and not making a decision at all. We stay where we are because it's safer, there's no risk involved. Unfortunately this waiting leaves us unfulfilled, wondering "What if...?"

The good news is that life doesn't work like that. If you want to move forward, that means understanding – and accepting – the fact that you're going to get it wrong. You're probably going to get it wrong quite often. The important thing is that you learn from those mistakes, and use that learning to propel you on to the next challenge. If you can train yourself to regard failure as an opportunity for growth, then you will eventually welcome failure because it's a sign that you are making progress – you're moving forwards.

Dealing with fear is another important skill to acquire, and – just like all the others – it's one that takes practice. For most of us, our biggest fears are to do with appearing vulnerable to other people – whether that is speaking in public, worrying about a physical challenge of some sort, or dealing with an uncomfortable atmosphere at home with our loved ones. We are reluctant to take the first step, for fear of embarrassment, rejection, or a host of other emotions that we'd rather avoid. I wish I could tell you there was a hack for this – a way to suddenly break through and make it all easy … unfortunately, there isn't. In her excellent book 'Daring Greatly', Brené Brown talks about how being vulnerable is actually a sign of courage, not weakness. Only by being vulnerable can we make real, meaningful progress.

It ultimately comes back to your comfort zone. You need to get out of it. The thing that most scares you is probably the thing you most need to do.

"Courage is resistance to fear, mastery of fear – not the absence of fear." Mark Twain, USA, 19th Century

> **'The Man in the Arena' [1910]**
> *Theodore Roosevelt*
> SUMMARY: An extraordinary speech, part of which deals with facing challenges.
> KEY QUOTE: "The credit belongs to the man who is actually in the arena."
>
> The title of Brené Brown's book is taken from a speech Theodore Roosevelt gave in Paris, formally called 'Citizenship in a Republic'. The most relevant passage for us is:
>
> *"It is not the critic who counts; not the man who points out how the strong man stumbles, or where the doer of deeds could have done them better. The credit belongs to the man who is actually in the arena, whose face is marred by dust*

and sweat and blood; who strives valiantly; who errs, who comes short again and again, because there is no effort without error and shortcoming ... (the man) who at the best knows in the end the triumph of high achievement, and who at the worst, if he fails, at least fails while daring greatly so that his place shall never be with those cold and timid souls who neither know victory nor defeat."

This idea of being in the arena is true in every area of our lives, from raising children, to entering your first 5km run, to giving up smoking. If you're in the arena, it's very easy for people to criticise and judge (especially on social media) ... but it's crucial that you do not attach too much importance to their opinions. If you are taking personal responsibility, staying true to your values and pursuing your goals, then no-one else's views matter. Hopefully you will get support from your loved ones – but sometimes even the people closest to you may struggle to understand the journey you are on.

When things get tough – and they always do – constantly remind yourself that "it is not the critic who counts".

"When men speak ill of thee, live so as nobody may believe them." Plato, Greek philosopher, 4th century BCE

MORE LIKE THIS: 'I Have a Dream' by Martin Luther King Jr, 'Nobel Acceptance Speech' by William Faulkner

WHEN TO QUIT

"If you don't like something, change it. If you can't change it, change your attitude." Maya Angelou, 20th century American writer

All the successful leaders we read about and listen to will tell you that in the middle of the night, when it's just them and the voices in their head, they have their doubts – are they doing the right thing, making the right decisions? The fear of failure is inside us all. It never goes away.

The fear of failure is closely related to the mantra 'winners never quit.' On one level, the idea that 'winners never quit' is absolutely true. If you give up every time life gets challenging, you are probably destined for a life of mediocrity. But there's another level here – continually banging your head against a brick wall isn't going to produce results either. Sometimes, you *do* need to quit. Sometimes, you need to realise that what you thought was a great idea … isn't. And at that point, it's time to take a breath, remind yourself where you're trying to get to, and look for a different solution – an alternative route to the top of the mountain.

> **'When to Quit'**
> *Chris Guillebeau, via Chase Jarvis, via Tim Ferriss*
> SUMMARY: A process for figuring out whether you need to change direction.
> KEY QUOTE: "Winners understand when and why to quit."
>
> Ferriss' podcast is one of my favourites. They are usually quite lengthy, so are great for listening to while walking the dog, or on long journeys. Episode #254 is entitled 'When To Quit', and features extracts from his interviews with Seth Godin, Debbie Millman, and a few others. My favourite section was from Chase Jarvis, photographer for Nike, Apple, Google, etc etc, and co-founder and CEO of CreativeLive (another fantastic learning resource).
>
> Jarvis discusses two ways to make decisions about when to quit. The first is very simple. He trusts his gut. Our intuition has fascinated scientists and thinkers for thousands of years, and it's something we can all relate to. You can probably think of a few times in your life when you trusted your instincts, and it proved to be the right decision … and there's probably also a few times when you went against

your gut, and it didn't work out too well. There is some early stage scientific research that suggests our intuition is actually part of our brain accessing stored information incredibly quickly, so it may be that our 'sixth sense' is just as real as the other five – we just haven't quite figured it out yet. (It's worth mentioning at this point that in the same way our eyes and ears can occasionally mislead us, no one is suggesting that our intuition is perfect, and to be trusted all the time!).

The second system Jarvis uses is to ask himself two questions:
1. IS THIS STILL WORKING? Am I moving forward, getting better, making progress?
2. DO I STILL CARE? Do I still believe in this? Do I love it?

When you've been working hard at something for a while and not quite getting the results you were expecting, these two questions can really help. If both your answers are 'yes', then obviously you should keep going. If you answer 'no' to both ... well, then it's time to get rid. If you get a yes and a no, then you need to dig deeper, but at least you've now got some information to work with. If you answered 'no' to question one, then you can look at the practicalities of why it's not working and find a solution. If you answered 'no' to the second question, then that's a bit trickier. Maybe it's time to check your values are still aligned correctly? Either way, asking these questions at least gives you a framework to then work towards a solution.

Incidentally, this incredibly valuable knowledge is a great example of how ideas get shared. The two questions are variations on an original idea from Chris Guillebeau (and I wouldn't be surprised if he originally learned them from someone else), who passed them on to Jarvis, who talked about them

> with Ferriss, which is where I found them, and have now passed them on to you. Who could you share this information with? Do you know someone who is stuck in a bit of a dead end, and could do with a way to make a better decision? Who can you help?
>
> *"It is not the blowing of the wind but the setting of the sails that will determine our direction in life." Jim Rohn, 20th century American author*

CONCLUSION

Like many of the ideas in this book, stepping up to lead is hard. Deciding to put yourself in the arena may feel like it's not worth the effort – and sometimes, it won't be. Maybe you volunteered to coach a sports team, or helped out at a local community centre – and it didn't really work out. It ended up being more trouble than it was worth. All you got was hassle, and you ended up feeling unappreciated and resenting making the effort in the first place. If that sounds familiar, remember what we've said about a personal responsibility, and having a growth mindset ... If you've had a negative experience with a leadership position, take a few moments to think about why it ended up that way. Is there anything you could have done differently? What can you learn from that experience?

It takes practice to become a good leader. We can discuss it, and you can go on to read another dozen books on the subject, but in the end you have to get out there and start doing it. And as you do, you'll get better at it. You'll have clear values and goals that you use to make decisions. You'll get better at communicating those ideas to the people around you – and listening to their ideas and feedback. Your ability to inspire the people around you will develop and grow, just like any other skill that you take time to practise. But perhaps more than any other, it's one where you have to get your hands dirty. You have to step up, and decide to lead.

CHAPTER 7 :: Leadership

Eventually you'll find something you care about so much that all the little niggles and challenges will seem unimportant. You can see a bigger picture – an area where you can make a real impact – and that will drive you forward. Whether that is turning around the fortunes of your local football club, directing a play for the first time, raising the money to build a school in India, or whatever your dream might be … eventually you will find something that gets a hold of you and won't let go, and you will make a difference.

But it won't happen if you sit on the sofa waiting for it. Go and get in the arena.

"Courage is the first of human qualities because it is the quality which guarantees the others." Aristotle, Greek philosopher, 4th century BCE

CHAPTER 8 :: TOOLS & TACTICS

INTRODUCTION

WE'RE ALMOST AT THE POINT where you need to start thinking about what you're going to do next, so in this chapter we'll be looking at the Tools and Tactics you might want to use moving forward.

The first thing to say is that we're all different – what works for me may not work for you, and that is absolutely fine. Try things out, and see what gives you the best results. Not all of it will speak to you. If you love 'The Secret', you might not enjoy reading the Stoics. Similarly, if you like the research-based approach of 'Mindset', then the story-based approach of 'Richest Man in Babylon' might not connect in the same way. Timing is likely to be important here – there is no question that a resource has to find you at the right time (see Gary Vaynerchuk on P80). Your mental state can also make a huge difference. Some days you need practical advice, others you need a bit of love ... and there will also be days when you need a kick in the backside! Pick your resources accordingly.

This is a good time to briefly mention again the importance of having a growth mindset, rather than a fixed mindset. When we have a growth mindset, we understand that with effort, we can improve anything and everything. At the beginning of your self-development journey you're going to need to demonstrate patience and perseverance as you work out the tools and tactics that work best for you. Keep an open mind until you have experienced and tested something for yourself.

HEALTH

"If you're in a bad mood, go for a walk. If you're still in a bad mood, go for another walk." Hippocrates, Greek physician, 5th century BCE

Your personal development starts here – without good health, everything else suffers. We all know that. This doesn't mean you have to be spending two hours in the gym every day and shifting to a Paleo diet (Google it if you're not sure), but it does mean you need to pay attention to your health. No one else can do it for you.

If we're honest with ourselves, most of us already have a fairly good idea how we're doing on the health front. If it's something that you need to work on, then I'm afraid it's beyond the scope of this book to get into specifics – but I do have some advice and suggestions. Firstly, everything in moderation is a pretty good starting point – put the Golden Mean (see P40) into practice. Completely cutting out alcohol or sugar is great, and will definitely improve your health – but it's also a really hard thing to do! If you know there's an area where you have a tendency to over-indulge, then start by cutting down rather than cutting out, and take it from there.

US Olympic gymnastic coach Christopher Sommer recommends changing your language around health. Forget 'diet and exercise', and think 'eat and train' instead. Ignore the latest fad diet from a glossy magazine, and focus on eating well every day so you have more energy. Don't think about exercising. Instead, focus on training your body so you are able to consistently perform at a higher level for longer. Shifting the language like this won't work for everyone, but it might help you start some new habits.

Knowing where to start can be tricky – there is so much advice out there about what you should or shouldn't eat, whether running is better for you than strength training, and so on ... but don't let this confusion be your excuse for not making the effort. Try something that instinctively makes sense for you and assess the results for yourself. If it doesn't

CHAPTER 8 :: Tools & Tactics

seem to be working, move on to something else. Just don't give up on yourself. Accept that it's going to involve work on your part, and understand that looking after your body is about the long-term effects – there are no quick fixes when it comes to your health. A simple process you can use (which can apply equally well to areas other than health) is the Triple A:

1. ACT :: Decide what you're going to do, and then begin. Don't procrastinate. Don't analyse it too much. Do 10 push ups. Go for a 15 minute walk. Anything. Just start.

2. ASSESS :: Measure your progress and regularly review the results. Is it working? Better or worse than you expected?

3. ADJUST :: What did you learn from your assessment? Make any changes, whether they are small modifications, or involve a complete change of direction.

Repeat these three steps over and over again, and you will make progress – but make sure you are constantly paying attention to your course. It's like driving – as you drive (take Action), you are always looking at the road conditions (Assessing), and tweaking the steering, changing your speed, using the brakes etc (Adjusting) in order to get to your destination. The road is rarely – if ever! – a straight line.

One last thing – please be patient and smart about this. Take medical advice before making any big changes to your eating or training habits, especially if you've not exercised for a few years.

BOOKS

Physical books are still my favourite tool, but that won't be true for everyone. And that's OK. If reading isn't your thing, that's fine – there are plenty of other resources you can turn to. But if you aren't a particularly keen reader to begin with, I'd really urge you to approach it with a growth mindset – it's like everything else; the more you do it, the better you'll get at it.

In the introduction I encouraged you to really personalise this book – highlight the bits that speak to you, make notes in the margins, use the inside of the covers to note your favourite pages, fold the corners down ... all the things we were told not to do at school! It's your book, so do what you want with it. Take this same approach with any other books you read. It serves two main purposes. The first is that highlighting passages helps them stick in your brain better. It also means you can come back to a book, skim it in just a few minutes and get all the best bits from it!

There are a couple of other things you might like to do. When you finish a book that has had a particular impact on you, make notes on it in your journal. Copying your favourite sentences down will really help the message and meaning sink in. The truth is that you may never refer back to those notes, but over time writing down important ideas by hand will have a cumulative positive affect on your thinking.

The other thing that is worth doing is learning to speed-read. It's actually not that hard. One basic technique for this is to use a pencil to guide your eye down the page line by line. Move the pencil faster, and you'll be surprised at how well your eyes can keep up. Another good thing to do is start and finish reading each line about four words from the edge of the page – you'll be surprised at how well your peripheral vision will pick up any important words. With a bit of practice, you can really improve the speed at which you read.

Your self-development starts with small steps, so set yourself a goal to read ten pages a day of a good book. At that rate you'll get through roughly a book a month, and that accumulated wisdom will quickly start to have a big impact on your life. If you don't know where to start, working through the list in the Appendix on P151 will introduce you to some of the classics, and the various different styles available to you.

AUDIO

There are two main resources here – audiobooks and podcasts, and both are excellent. Use them in the car, while you're exercising or out walking the dog. If you haven't got headphones, consider investing in a Bluetooth headset – my Plantronics M70 was only about £20, has been dropped more times than I remember, and is still going strong. I now walk round the supermarket listening to Shane Parrish or Radiotopia, and it's amazing!

The choice of audio available is a bit overwhelming, so my best advice is to look at the overall review score. If an audiobook or podcast has more than 50 reviews and it's getting a good score, you can be pretty confident in the quality. That doesn't necessarily mean you'll enjoy it, of course, but at least you're reducing the chance that it's a load of rubbish.

With audio, you can easily turn your commute, exercise routine or shopping trip into a core part of your self development. Think of your smartphone as your personal library and university course.

EMAIL

For a lot of people, their email inbox has become a huge distraction, full of so much junk and spam that the idea of going through it all is a bit of a nightmare. I have a suggestion for you – delete the whole lot. Seriously. When was the last time you re-read any emails from 2009? From last month, even?

I get that there might be some you want to keep for sentimental value or legal reasons, but 99% of emails can be deleted. Take the time to unsubscribe from any promotional stuff you don't read – legally, there has to be a link in every message – it takes seconds to find and click through. Next, adopt a 'One Touch' response to any new emails that arrive. You've got four options: action it, file it, delegate it, bin it. Whichever option you decide is appropriate, do it there and then – with 'One Touch' – don't leave it until later unless you really have to. To help with this, switch off any email notifications you get, and set specific times to keep up to date with your email. Two or three times a day is plenty – and many of us can probably manage on once a day. How many truly important emails do you really get each day?

BLOGS

The last step in making your email inbox more interesting is to visit some blogs and spend a few minutes subscribing to some newsletters that you might actually enjoy receiving! Plenty of smart, interesting people out there are curating newsletters that aren't just full of cat GIFs. I've mentioned several in the book, including Seth Godin, Shane Parrish and Tim Urban. Others you might enjoy are Brain Pickings for in depth book reviews, Austin Kleon for creative inspiration, Finimise for financial nuggets, or … just get out there and start looking! And don't forget to unsubscribe if something ends up not being your thing.

VIDEO

It is staggering how much amazing content is out there for free, and this is particularly true of video content. Your first stop here is TED, which I have already mentioned several times. Substitute 30 minutes a day of mindless TV for a TED talk or two, and in just a few days you could have absorbed Ken Robinson on education, Elizabeth Gilbert on creativity, Dan Pink on motivation, and Monica Lewinsky on shame. And that's just for starters. Everything on TED is high quality – it might not all speak to you (you get that by now, right?!) but anything with 10 million or more views will be worth watching.

YouTube is the other obvious place to go – but it's a lot more hit and miss. (There's also a much bigger risk of falling into a wormhole that ends up four hours later at 'The 100 Best Cat Fails EVER!!!!!!!!'). If you need a kick in the backside, there's some good motivational stuff from Mateusz M and Be Inspired, other than that, my only real advice is to search a person like Tony Robbins or Tim Ferriss, and see what you find. There will be a lot of rubbish, so make sure you're disciplined about skipping videos that aren't doing anything for you.

ONLINE COURSES

A more reliable source for good video content is an online learning resource like Udemy or CreativeLive (where you usually have to pay). You've also got Khan Academy or Coursera, which are both free. The choice of courses available now is staggering – almost a bit overwhelming – so I'd recommend visiting these sites with a specific purpose in mind, rather than just browsing and seeing what takes your fancy. If you go looking for a 'Photography' course, the choice will be endless. But if you look for 'Travel Photography on an iPhone', you'll likely get something much more useful.

If you're looking for somewhere to start, 'Learning How to Learn' on Coursera is interesting, useful, short, and free.

PEOPLE

We become the average of the five people we spend the most time with. We tend to earn roughly the same, have similar opinions, and like the same things as the people we see most often. We can choose to have this principle work for us, or against us.

Think of the people you know that lift you up. After you've spent time with them you feel invigorated, energised and optimistic. Do you have people like this that you could see more often?

Now consider the people who have the opposite effect. After being in their company you feel depressed and lethargic. You may need to start spending less time with these people – and this might be tough to do. They might be family members, or friends you have had for many years. You don't necessarily need to cut them out of your life completely, but you might want to consider limiting the time you spend with them.

Use this principle of becoming the average of the five people you hang out with to your advantage. Think carefully about who you let in to your inner circle. If you want to get healthier, then you need to spend time with people who don't live on pizza and takeaways. If you want to earn more money, find ways to meet people who earn more than you and see what you can learn from them.

Make the effort to get out into the world and see who you can find to talk to. There are lots of different ways to do this – whether it's joining a local club, or attending an international conference (see below for more on events). When you do this, be sure you understand the difference between networking, which is meeting people with the specific intention of doing business with them, and socialising, which is about having a sense of belonging with people you can rely on and turn to for help and advice. There is obviously some overlap between the two (it's fine to be friends with people you do business with!), but be clear on the difference.

In either case, remember that when you meet a new person there is a three-stage process of Know, Like, and Trust to go through. First, someone has to get to know you a bit. Hopefully they will then like you, and if they do, they may eventually get to the point where they trust you. You can't rush this, or manipulate it – people see through that sort of insincerity in seconds. Be yourself, act with integrity, and see where it takes you.

EVENTS

When the time comes to start expanding your social, community and business networks, there are a number of different routes you can take. There might be some local talks you can attend, or a bigger event like TEDx (there are a surprising number of these events going on all over the world – see the TED website for more info). Depending on what you do for a living, you might find a business networking

CHAPTER 8 :: Tools & Tactics

group makes sense for you to attend.

Once you find yourself at an event, it's important to try and make the most of it. If you know there are going to be speakers of some sort, make sure you've got a way to take notes. Try to take advantage of the before and after opportunities – arrive early, see who else is there, and strike up a conversation. For many people, talking to strangers like this will be outside your comfort zone and so is self–development in itself! If that sounds like you, then the acronym FORM might help. It's a good way to start – and maintain – a conversation with someone you've never met before:

- **F**ROM :: Where are they based? Do they live locally? Have they been there long?

- **O**CCUPATION :: What do they do for a living? Do they enjoy it? How long have they done it for?

- **R**ECREATION :: What do they do in their spare time? How did they get interested in that?

- **M**OTIVATION :: Ask 'why' to any of their other answers. i.e. What made you decide to move out of London? Did you always want to be a teacher? Did you play football as a kid, or was it something you got into later?

Conversation is a skill just like any other – practise it, and you'll get better. You'll also meet some interesting people this way!

MENTORING

Mentoring can take many different forms, but basically boils down to having a person more experienced than you in a certain area that you turn to for guidance and advice. This may happen in 'real life' – perhaps you strike up a conversation with the speaker at an event, and that person becomes your mentor. To start with though, your mentors are more likely to be 'virtual' – the people who produce the writing, video and audio that you learn from. It's a bit of a one-sided relationship, in that you don't often get a chance to speak with these people ... having said that, there are plenty of stories of tweets or emails being responded to, so hit your mentors up on social media – you never know your luck!

COACHING

Coaching is a bit different to mentoring – primarily because it's something you will pay for. For many years, I was completely comfortable with the idea of having a coach to help me learn the drums, or get better at a sport – but the idea of having someone 'coach' me in how to live a better life seemed ludicrous.

Why should that be? I think one of the main reasons is that the results are harder to measure. If you have a running coach, after a few weeks or months you'll know whether it's working or not because you'll see your 5km 'personal best' time start to come down. Measuring progress in your life is a lot more difficult! If this seems like something you'd like to try, then meet up with a potential coach and ask questions. Be open to coaching opportunities, but don't throw your money at the first person you meet. Especially if they say they can "transform your life in ten days, or your money back!"

MEDITATION

In all the research I did for this book, meditation was mentioned in one form or another by almost every writer. Some of them cite it as essential, some of them as a useful technique ... but pretty much everybody in the world of self-development agrees that meditation is a good idea.

This doesn't necessarily mean sitting in lotus position with incense burning and panpipe music playing! (Although there's nothing wrong with that if it works for you). At its most basic, 'meditating' is nothing more than taking a few moments to stop, remove distractions, and focus on yourself. There are an unlimited number of variations on this theme, and – like a lot of things – if you've never done it before, the idea of meditating can be daunting.

The most basic meditation practice (and note they are called 'practices' – the more you do them, the better you get) is to just sit comfortably, with your back straight, and breathe deeply. As you breathe, focus on the air coming in and how it makes you feel – be aware of any aches and pains, then softly let the air out. Repeat for a few minutes. That's pretty much it!

Another relatively simple practice is the 'loving–kindness' meditation. Sit comfortably, and take a few deep breaths to get relaxed. Then bring to mind someone close to you, and for a minute or so just wish them happiness in their day. Repeat this for two more people.

One of the biggest misconceptions with meditation is that you are somehow trying to 'empty' your mind. This isn't quite accurate. You are trying to free your mind from distractions – but that is virtually impossible! So, as you breathe, try to notice when you get distracted – whether it is the sound of a car going by, or the thought of what's for dinner, notice the thought, then gently bring your focus back to your breathing.

Each time you bring your focus back, you are meditating successfully. As you practice, you will find you get distracted less and less, but don't beat yourself up in the beginning. In the same way as you don't go from the sofa to running a marathon in a week, you won't achieve a perfect Zen state after a few days of deep breathing!

If you're interested in learning more, try an app like Headspace or Calm, which have guided meditations you can use to get started. Authors to consider include Sharon Salzberg and Tara Brach.

JOURNALING

"Without knowing the force of words, it is impossible to know more." Confucius, Chinese philosopher, 6th century BCE

"A word after a word after a word is power." Margaret Atwood, 20th century Canadian writer

Cliche time again: a short pencil is better than a long memory.

Like almost everything in this book, the importance of journaling is something that I've heard repeated by everybody from Napoleon Hill to Tony Robbins. You already know what I'm going to say – if it's good enough for those guys, then maybe the rest of us need to do it too. Repeated time and again is the message that there is power in physically committing words to paper. Digital versions don't seem to have the same effect. Evernote and the like are good for keeping track of lists and research … but the personal stuff – the really important stuff – needs to be handwritten, by you.

First and foremost, journaling is different to keeping a diary. While part of your journal can be keeping track of what you did, where you went, and who you saw on a particular day, it's much more than that. It's the place you keep track of your goals, dreams, ideas and inspiration – of the things that really mean something to you.

For me personally, the amount I write each day varies enormously, so I use a blank notebook. My journal is a big part of my morning routine (see P87). I start each day on a new page with the date and a list of three things that I am grateful for. Next, I write down Today's Top Three things to do and three affirmations.

Then I write about how I'm feeling. Sometimes this is just a sentence or two, but if I'm feeling a little stuck for some reason, I will do a 'Stream of Consciousness' passage. The term was first used by psychologist William James in 1890, and relates to the idea that thoughts are continually running through our minds. At times, it can be hard to see the connections between all these thoughts – and at other times they seem overwhelming. In either case, getting them down on paper is a good way to make some sense of it.

Just write. You're not worrying about spelling, or grammar, or even making any sense! Just write continuously, for as long as it takes for your mind to start clearing. Sometimes this will be a few minutes, but you might have to write for 15–20 minutes before your brain starts to calm down. The most important thing is to not stop. Don't re-read any of it, don't pause to think about what you want to write next – just write. It sounds a bit nuts, but you might be surprised at how much it helps.

Throughout the day, I try to keep my journal to hand and add things to it if they feel relevant. I don't take it everywhere, so will sometimes make a note in my phone that gets transferred to my journal later if I'm out and about.

I try to always go back to my journal last thing at night. I will jot down any thoughts I've had, list three brilliant things that happened today, and finish with 'Tomorrow's Top Three' – the three most important things that I need to get done tomorrow.

Your journal is – of course – entirely personal to you. I like to be disciplined with it, as I find it helps me get the day off to a good start. But you may find that you prefer to get stuck in to your day, and spending time journaling first thing slows you down. Experiment, and see what suits you best.

UNDERSTANDING WHY

"He who has a why to live can bear almost any how." Friedrich Nietzsche, 19th century German philosopher

There are two types of 'why' question that we need to answer. The first is "why am I doing this?", and this is related to your Values and Goals, which we have already covered. The second question we may have to ask ourselves is "why is this not going the way I expected it to?". This one is generally easier to answer than the first, but we still need to spend time with it.

A good system to use is the 'Five Whys', most closely associated with Sakichi Toyoda of the Toyota car company. Let's say you have set yourself the goal of losing 6kgs in six months, but after two months you're a bit behind schedule. Instead of getting down on yourself (which will probably lead to your giving up on the goal), ask yourself why you are not on target. If the reason is that you've only been to the gym once or twice a week instead of the three times you intended, ask yourself why. Do you find you keep running out of time? Again, why is that? Keep digging, keep asking yourself why. Each answer forms the basis of the next question. This 'chained why' approach helps you get below the surface and into the real underlying reasons something is happening. You want to get to the root cause, rather than responding to the symptoms.

This isn't just about addressing challenges. It's also useful to apply this system to things that go better than you expected. If you lost those 6kgs in just five months instead of six, why was that? Are there any ideas that you can apply to help you succeed in other areas of your life?

POSITIVE MENTAL ATTITUDE

"The most important decision you make is to be in a good mood."
Voltaire, 18th century French philosopher

"We lost because we told ourselves we lost." Leo Tolstoy, 19th century Russian author

For many people, the concept of positive mental attitude (PMA) conjures up images of whooping and cheering crowds, all high–fiving and slapping each other on the back … while completely ignoring the realities of life. Thankfully, there is a bit more to it than that.

There is little doubt that our attitude has a huge impact on our lives. "The soul becomes dyed by the colour of its thoughts", wrote Marcus Aurelius. A famous Buddhist saying is: "All that we are arises with our thoughts." Unfortunately, a lot of the time quotes like these are taken out of their original context, which can leave people with the idea that it's enough to just think deeply about something in order for it to happen. But as Napoleon Hill points out:

> *"First comes thought; then organisation of that thought, into ideas and plans; then transformation of those plans into reality. The beginning, as you will observe, is in your imagination."*

CHAPTER 8 :: Tools & Tactics

While our imagination might be where things start, Hill makes it clear that thoughts alone are not enough – there needs to be planning, and then *doing* before anything will actually happen.

Of course, if we flip that around and just start 'doing' before we plan without giving any thought to what we really want, then it's extremely unlikely that we will end up where we intended. Going back to the holiday analogy we used earlier. Firstly, you have to decide where you want to go, and when – you need to think about what you want. Then you plan the logistics of the trip. It's only once we have these details in place that we actually take action and begin the journey. Imagine the opposite. If you just walk out the door one morning without any thought or planning, then yes, there's a chance you'll end up on a beautiful beach in the Seychelles … but there's a much bigger chance that you won't.

Now let's take this a step further, and consider our attitude when we initially start thinking about going on that holiday. We could take the 'woe is me' approach, and be negative about everything. "Oh, it's so expensive, we'll never be able to save that much. And I probably won't get the time off work. And we've got to find someone to feed the cat … It's going to be more trouble than it's worth." Or, we can choose to have a positive attitude. "Yes, it's a lot of money and it's going to be a challenge to save up, but we're going to remember these two weeks for the rest of our lives. It's going to be the best holiday ever!" You don't have to be an ancient Greek philosopher to work out which approach is likely to give you better results.

We aren't talking about mindless optimism here. When life lays down a challenge, it doesn't help to pretend it's not there. But it *does* help if you face that situation with courage, and the belief that you can find a solution. Walking through life with your head in the clouds won't get you anywhere, but realistic positivity will, and it starts in your head.

This idea is commonly seen in sports. Speak to any

contemporary sportsperson, and they will tell you that visualisation of their goals is an important part of their mental training ... but equally, Usain Bolt did not win all those gold medals by just dreaming about it. For decades, he also had intense daily training sessions on the running track.

Anyone who has achieved something physical that the rest of us might see as 'superhuman' – walking to the South Pole, summiting Everest, or running a sub–3–hour marathon – will tell you it's a mental battle as much as a physical one. The same thing often happens when people have children. They suddenly find they can function on limited, intermittent sleep, when previously they 'needed' eight hours sleep a night.

A famous example of overcoming this mental barrier is Roger Bannister running the four-minute mile in 1954. Most people felt this was simply beyond the physical capabilities of the human body. But once Bannister had demonstrated it was possible, 15 other runners got below four minutes by the end of 1957. Bannister proved it wasn't physical. He believed he could do it when no-one else did. He had a positive mental attitude.

These ideas are integral to one of the more controversial areas of personal development – the Law of Attraction (LOA). The LOA states that whatever you think about, comes about. For example, if you want a new car, you need to get yourself into the mindset where you truly believe you already own that car. LOA advocates believe that thinking about what you want is enough to achieve all your wildest dreams. Running alongside this is the idea that when bad things happen to you, it's because you have 'attracted' them into your life. At its most extreme, this principle is applied to everything from financial success ("she believed she would get rich, so she is") to getting ill ("he thought negative thoughts, so he attracted it into his life").

There is little doubt that what goes on in your head is massively important. When everything else is equal, having a positive attitude is way better than having a negative attitude.

Exactly how far attitude can take a person before they have to start putting some work in is more debatable. As always, I would encourage you to make your own mind up.

> **'The Secret' [2006]**
> *Rhonda Byrne*
> SUMMARY: Short, easy to read and inspirational book about implementing the Law of Attraction.
> KEY QUOTE: "There is a truth deep down inside of you that has been waiting for you to discover it, and that truth is this: you deserve all good things life has to offer."
>
> This is the best known of the books about the Law of Attraction, selling millions of copies worldwide in the couple of years after release. I first read it a long time ago on a beach in Egypt because I'd run out of things to read. I opened it full of cynicism, expecting to hate every page ... but ... instead, I found it very thought-provoking.
>
> The biggest issue I had – and still have – with 'The Secret' is that it gives the reader the impression that all you have to do is think positive thoughts, and somehow the universe will align to bring you everything you need, from a parking space, to the house of your dreams, to the perfect partner. Leaving the dodgy pseudo-science to one side, at no point does the book say anything about doing any work – but interestingly when you research the people quoted in the book, you discover that they have worked hard to get to where they are. Even the book itself and accompanying film came about as a result of six months hard work. But none of this is mentioned in the text.
>
> Whatever you might end up thinking about this book it's an important one to read, because ultimately you need to draw your own conclusions about it. I have met people who swear that their

life turned around after they started using the Law of Attraction … and I've also met people that are enraged by what they see as hokum, cashing in on people's desire for a quick fix. It can seem like the Law of Attraction is the spiritual equivalent of winning the Lottery.

'The Secret' will likely stir strong feelings one way or the other in you, and that is exactly why you should read it. Whether you end up loving it or hating it, I urge you to approach it in the first instance with an open, curious and – most importantly – questioning mind.

"Nurture great thoughts, for you will never go higher than your thoughts." Benjamin Disraeli, 19th century British statesman

"Whether you think you can, or think you can't, either way you are right." Henry Ford, 20th century American industrialist

MORE LIKE THIS: There isn't really anything else quite like 'The Secret' – if you want to know more about the Law of Attraction, this is the one to read. If you like it, a couple of books that are stylistically similar are 'Chicken Soup for the Soul' by Jack Canfield & Mark Victor Hansen, and 'The Top Five Regrets of the Dying' by Bronnie Ware.

A WORD OF WARNING!

The things we've talked about in this chapter are tools – make sure you are using them, and not the other way around. Be careful not to convince yourself that spending two hours online 'researching' great blogs is a substitute for actually taking action. An hour a day on this stuff is plenty – by all means do more, but only if everything else is on target.

One last thing – reading inspirational memes on social media doesn't count as personal development. As the saying goes, "it's never your successful friends posting the inspirational quotes."

> **'Tools of Titans' [2016]**
> *Tim Ferriss*
> SUMMARY: Succinct advice from world-class performers that we can all use.
> KEY QUOTE: "Borrow liberally, combine uniquely, and create your own bespoke blueprint."
>
> Ferriss hosts one of the most popular podcasts in the world. He conducts long-form interviews lasting anywhere from 1-3 hours (yes, hours!) with people who are world-renowned experts in their field, whether that is health, science, business, or whatever. You may not be familiar with all his guests, but the quality is universally excellent and Ferriss always seems to find a way to really dig into the details.
>
> I highly recommend the podcast – but each episode is a little commitment. You can't really skip through the interviews, as you don't know which bits will resonate with you. To help with this, his book 'Tools of Titans' is a brilliant introduction to the type of people he talks to, and what they talk about.
>
> The book is essentially edited highlights from the podcast. Over 100 guests are included, but each one only gets a few pages. Ferriss introduces each person with a short bio so you get a sense of who they are and what they've done, and then summarises some of the best bits from that person's interview.
>
> It's over 600 pages, but don't let that put you off. Because each person only gets a couple of pages, you can easily dip into it for a few minutes at a time. Think of it like a buffet dinner – you can pick and choose what you want to consume. The book is divided into three sections – healthy, wealthy, and wise – and the quality of intelligent thinking and practical advice it contains is truly exceptional.

One little bit of advice. It starts with the 'Healthy' section, and some of the early interviews dig into some quite detailed scientific analysis of different diets and eating habits. Don't let that put you off! Read the introduction to the book, then just open it at random, and see who and what you discover ...

"Bernard of Chartres used to say that we [the Moderns] are like dwarves perched on the shoulders of giants [the Ancients], and thus we are able to see more and farther than the latter. And this is not at all because of the acuteness of our sight or the stature of our body, but because we are carried aloft and elevated by the magnitude of the giants." John of Salisbury, 12th century English philosopher

MORE LIKE THIS: 'A Calendar of Wisdom' by Leo Tolstoy, 'The 100 Best Business Books of All Time' by Jack Covert & Todd Sattersten

CHAPTER 9 :: NEXT STEPS

"The best time to plant a tree was 20 years ago. The second best time is now." Chinese proverb

"Living is not breathing, but doing." Jean-Jaques Rousseau, 18th century Genevan philosopher

"You are what you do, not what you say you do." Carl Jung, 20th century Swiss psychiatrist

IF YOU'VE GOT THIS FAR, the chances are that at least some of the ideas have resonated with you, and you're now wondering what to do next. The great thing is there is no right or wrong answer to this. Hopefully a couple of the resource summaries have sparked an interest for you. Start there. Invest in a couple of second-hand books from Amazon. Read the first chapter – if you like it, keep going. If not, put it to one side and try a different author.

If reading isn't your thing right now, watch a TED talk (start with their top ten most viewed), or listen to a podcast (try Tim Ferriss, Chase Jarvis or Gary Vaynerchuk).

Once you start looking, you'll quickly discover what works for you. Don't forget that different personalities will connect with different people at different times. Remember the Chinese proverb: "When the student is ready, the teacher will appear."

This has been true for me countless times. The most striking example was with Gary Vaynerchuk. The first time I heard him on a Facebook Live, I thought he was the biggest jerk on the planet – a loud-mouthed, obnoxious salesman with no real depth, and nothing to offer. I don't really know why I went back to him, but a couple of years after that initial contact I downloaded a couple of his podcasts.

BAM!

It was like being struck by lightning. I had changed in those intervening years, and now, his message and delivery was exactly what I needed. His no-nonsense approach cut through the haze, and made me face the reality of my procrastination and excuse-making.

You will have similar experiences. No-one can predict which books or speakers will have the most impact on you – but someone out there is saying what you need to hear.

If you haven't already, then it's time to get started. Right now. Flick back through the chapters and order a book or two. Visit ted.com. Download a few podcast episodes. Subscribe to a couple of blogs. If you want a plan, Appendix 1 on P149 has a list of ten simple actions to get you started.

Who knows … it could change your life.

"You don't have to see the whole staircase. Just take the first step."
Martin Luther King Jr, 20th century American activist

SELF-HELP TO HELP THE WORLD

"A man wrapped up in himself makes a very small bundle." Benjamin Franklin, 18th century American polymath

"Act as if what you do makes a difference. It does." William James, 19th century American philosopher

HOPEFULLY BY NOW YOU'VE GOT a few ideas about some changes you want to start implementing in your life, and how you're going to go about doing some of those things. That's brilliant – and is the whole point of this book. The last thing I want to do is overwhelm you right at the end, but there's one other really important thing you need to know about self-education and personal development.

It's not about you.

It's about what you can *do* – the impact you can have … the difference you can make for other people.

The world is full of people that need our help. By starting your personal development journey, you are starting a process whereby you can be more and do more than you ever thought possible. This starts with the people immediately around you – your friends and family. Then as you develop and progress, this can spread further and further

CHAPTER 9 :: Next Steps

– your 'Circle of Influence' (remember that?! See P25) gets bigger and bigger, and the difference you can make increases too. One of the most exciting and fulfilling parts of self-development is the realisation that you can truly make a difference to the world.

This can be hard to grasp at first – the negative self-talk gets louder, you feel you're getting 'too big for your boots', that you don't have the skills … all of these doubts can hold us back. But when you do step out of your comfort zone and into the arena, a remarkable thing happens. You almost won't realise it to start, but gradually you'll notice little things changing. A comment on Facebook doesn't wind you up the way it used to … you are a bit more patient with people … you find it easier to say no to things you don't want to do … and these turn into big things – you feel happier, less stressed, and more fulfilled …

It will happen. If you do the work, it will happen.

And when it does, start to share with people. This may feel uncomfortable at first, but you can start with recommending a podcast, or giving your favourite book to someone at Christmas. Or just share your time with people – make the effort to really listen to someone with a problem, or do an unexpected favour for someone. The sharing is an important part of the process. There's a selfish element – you'll feel better as a result, but that's not why we do it. We do it because helping other people is the right thing to do.

"Everything that lives, lives not alone, nor for itself." William Blake, 18th century English poet

"Never worry about numbers. Help one person at a time and always start with the person nearest you." Mother Teresa, 20th century Albanian–Indian missionary

"I looked around for somebody to do something. Then I realised I am somebody." Unknown

WHY BOTHER?

Hopefully, it won't have escaped your attention that many times throughout this book I've mentioned how much work is involved in personal development. So it's an entirely reasonable question to ask – why bother?

What if you *don't* bother?

What does your life look like in ten years if you put these ideas to one side, and don't make any changes?

The main argument for going through the self-development process revolves around the number of smart, successful (in the broadest possible sense of the word) people who have made the journey before us. The realisation that so many of the people I admire, from Lao Tzu to Tim Urban, have bothered to spend time thinking about what it really means to live a good life, to be a good person, to leave the world a better place … that realisation made me think that there must be a reason why all these wise people bother to put the effort in – there must be *something* in this personal development malarky.

And there undoubtedly is. When I think back to that day when I looked in the mirror and asked myself "How did I end up here?", somewhere deep inside me was a sense that I could be and do more. That I hadn't yet fulfilled my potential. I still haven't. In fact, I think I've still got an awfully long way to go … but I've definitely started the journey, and it's thanks to the people and ideas in this book.

If you've read this far, then I suspect that somewhere deep inside you know that you haven't yet fulfilled your potential, either. I don't know where your journey will take you – nobody does – but perhaps it is time for you to start making some changes?

"It does not matter how slowly you go, as long as you do not stop."
Confucius, China, 6th century BCE

> **'The Alchemist' [1988]**
> *Paulo Coelho*
> SUMMARY: A short fable about figuring out what is truly important.
> KEY QUOTE: "The simple things are also the most extraordinary things, and only the wise can see them."
>
> Over 30 million copies of this book have been sold worldwide – Coelho's simple, gentle style evidently speaks to something in lots of us. 'The Alchemist' is a parable about a young boy who goes in search of his dreams, and the lessons he learns along the way. It's a relatively short book, but one that contains an awful lot of wisdom. If you're looking for practical advice, this probably isn't the book for you – but if you're in a more thoughtful mood, then the metaphors it contains might be exactly what you're looking for.
>
> *"We shall not cease from exploration, and the end of all our exploring will be to arrive where we started and know the place for the first time." T.S. Eliot, 20th century American/English poet*
>
> MORE LIKE THIS: 'Illusions' by Richard Bach, 'The Prophet' by Kahlil Gibran

DO THE WORK

You're almost at the end, so the last thing I want to do is put you off taking the next step.

But I also don't want you operating under any false illusions – or (which would be worse), delusions.

If you want to change things, it is often quite simple. But simple things are not always easy.

There are going to be times when you will wonder if the effort is worth it. You'll question your decision when the people you've known for years start giving you funny looks as they notice you changing. When you start getting frustrated at work because you know you can make a bigger contribution – but can't seem to get your foot in the door anywhere else. When you slip back into an old, unhealthy habit that you thought you'd broken. When these challenges arise, you will need to look inside yourself – deep inside – and be prepared to find out who you really are.

Without doubt, it's easier to stay right where you are. But look five … ten … twenty years down the road … Do you want to be in the same place then as you are now? If not, you need to remember two simple truths:

1. Insanity is doing the same thing over and over and expecting different results. (Often misattributed to Einstein – no-one is too sure on it's actual origins).

2. For things to change, YOU have to change.

The path to changing isn't easy, and there aren't any shortcuts.

But … and it's a huge, important 'but' … I also promise you that it will be worth it.

It may well be that you love your life, and don't want to change anything. If that's you – then congratulations! You've nailed Life! But if you're still reading, then I'm guessing there are at least a couple of areas where you think things could be a bit better. If that's the case – then congratulations! You now know what needs to change.

You.

I'm excited for you – your journey to a new, improved version of you and your life is waiting for you.

Get focused on what you want.

Then go and do it.

"Your time is limited, so don't waste it living someone else's life." Steve Jobs, 20th century American entrepreneur

"You always chose to be bound by who you are. Now choose to be freed by who you are." Robin Hobb, 21st century American writer

APPENDIX 1 :: 10-POINT ACTION PLAN

THERE ARE A LOT OF different ideas in this book, many of which may be completely new to you. I remember well that feeling of being inspired … but at the same time not quite knowing where to begin. If that seems familiar, then I have some simple suggestions to get you started. Feel free to ignore some (or all!) of them, but making even a few of the following changes will pay dividends in the weeks, months and years ahead:

1. START YOUR JOURNAL. If you haven't already, then start paying closer attention to your life by writing about it. Even if it's just a couple of sentences a day, jot something down.

2. MORNING ROUTINE. Look at the list on P87, pick at least three that make sense to you, and start doing them every morning.

3. DECIDE ON YOUR VALUES. Spend five minutes writing a list of all the values that are important to you, then narrow it down to the top three. Start using them to guide your decisions.

4. SET SOME SMART GOALS. Start with three. A little one to be accomplished in the next couple of weeks. Another that might take 3–6 months to achieve, and a third that will take a couple of years. Review them daily.

5. PLAN YOUR WEEK. Start making time for the important people and tasks in your life. Prioritise your 'to do' list. What belongs on the 'not to do list'?

6. LISTEN. The next time someone comes to you with a problem, resolve to truly listen, don't just look for the gap where you can start speaking.

7. IMPROVE YOUR HEALTH. Start one small habit to improve your health. 10 push ups every morning. One less treat per day. Keep it simple and achievable in the early days.

8. USE A RESOURCE. Listen to a TED talk, download a podcast, order a book. (All three?)

9. IGNORE THE VOICES. The next time your brain starts trying to put you off, gently acknowledge it, but don't give it your attention.

10. TAKE ACTION!

There are lots of free downloads including a weekly planner, a chart for monitoring your habits, a goal–setting worksheet and much more at my website:
www.joeredston.com/shs/resources

You'll also find links to all the books, podcasts and other resources I have mentioned.

APPENDIX 2 :: 12 BOOKS TO GET YOU STARTED

READING TEN PAGES A DAY, you'll get through roughly a book a month. If you buy the following 12 books in the next 12 months, read them all cover to cover, and do nothing else, I guarantee you will be in a better place than you are now.

This list is predominantly the personal development classics – some will appeal more than others, and you might find that there are a couple you end up really disliking! However, reading these 12 titles will give you a more detailed look at the ideas contained within this book, and you will also get a sense of which style of personal development works best for you. (Always remember the comfort zone though – it's good to read outside of your emotional or intellectual comfort zone so you get a sense of the bigger picture).

There is – of course – no definitive opinion of what constitutes the 'best' in self education, so there is naturally a subjective element to this list:

1. 'Man's Search For Meaning', by Viktor Frankl
2. 'Mindset', by Dr Carol S. Dweck
3. 'The Richest Man in Babylon', by George S. Clason
4. 'The 7 Habits of Highly Effective People', by Stephen R. Covey
5. 'Portrait of an Extraordinary Man', by Richard Stengel
6. 'The Secret', by Rhonda Byrne
7. 'Tools of Titans', by Tim Ferriss
8. 'How to Win Friends and Influence People', by Dale Carnegie
9. 'Awaken The Giant Within', by Anthony Robbins
10. 'Think and Grow Rich', by Napoleon Hill

11. 'Start With Why', by Simon Sinek

12. 'The Alchemist', by Paulo Coelho

I'd suggest reading them in the order above, but feel free to start with 'The Alchemist' if you want to. I run a resources club at my website which has two options. The first is an occasional newsletter with reviews and recommendations of books, videos, podcasts etc that I've been enjoying.

Sign up at: www.joeredston.com/newsletter

The second option is to receive monthly emails about the books on this list. When you sign up, your first email contains a summary of 'Man's Search for Meaning', and a link to buy it. A month later you'll get an email about 'Mindset', a month after that will be 'Richest Man in Babylon', and so on. It's free to sign up, there's no obligation to purchase any of them, and you can unsubscribe at any time.

Join the book club at: www.joeredston.com/shs/12books

ABOUT THE AUTHOR

Joe currently lives on the beautiful Isle of Wight, just off the southern coast of England. After an eclectic start to his career, which included time as a musician and running the England beach soccer team, he now works in corporate team building. His company, Raise Global, combine leadership development with meaningful giving. When he's not working, reading, or travelling, you'll probably find Joe outside ... probably accompanied by his dog, Scout.

Discover more about Joe, including his blog and podcast at:
www.joeredston.com

Learn more about Raise at:
www.raise.global

ACKNOWLEDGEMENTS

The biggest and most important thanks go to Mum and Dad. You have both been there for me more times than I can remember over the years, and I can't thank you enough.

Fran - thank you for believing in me.

To my friends Andy and Rupert, your passion, humility and integrity are a constant source of inspiration.

To Mr Thatcher, for the (very!) early encouragement, and invaluable feedback.

Thanks to Jacey for your brilliant illustrations and endless coffees!

And to all the people I have learnt from over the years - especially the ones who have shown me a different way to be, I thank you.

One last story ... the day after I printed copies of the first draft of this book, I met somebody new - someone who soars in a way I have never experienced before. I want to say thank you to that extraordinary person ... and to remind anyone else reading this that you never, ever know what tomorrow will bring ...

45227658R00099

Printed in Poland
by Amazon Fulfillment
Poland Sp. z o.o., Wrocław